D0489986

THE TACTICS
OF THE RICH

**When it comes to creating wealth,
it ain't *what* you do,
it's the *way* that you do it!**

Paul A Overy QFA FLIA

Published by
OAK TREE PRESS
19 Rutland Street, Cork, Ireland
www.oaktreepress.com

© 2008 Paul Overy

A catalogue record of this book is
available from the British Library.

ISBN 978 1 904887 18 8 (pb)
ISBN 978 1 904887 19 5 (hb)

All rights reserved.
No part of this publication may be reproduced or transmitted
in any form or by any means, including photocopying and
recording, without written permission of the publisher. Such
written permission must also be obtained before any part of
this publication is stored in a retrieval system of any nature.
Requests for permission should be directed to
Oak Tree Press, 19 Rutland Street, Cork, Ireland.

Illustrations by Ken Lee.

Printed in Ireland by ColourBooks.

CONTENTS

INTRODUCTION

Very few of us know anything about money, about how to make investments, about tax or borrowing or risk management. It is this very lack of knowledge that has led, in my view, to "sound-bite" financial advice. Our parents, our teachers, our bankers or friends, all trot out these old stalwarts from time to time. Examples include:

- *"Money is the root of all evil."*
- *"Neither a borrower, nor a lender be."*
- *"Don't put all your eggs in one basket."*
- *"Look after the 'pennies' and the 'pounds' will look after themselves."*
- *"A bird in the hand is worth two in the bush."*
- *"Buy low, sell high."*
- *"Money makes money."*
- *"Money makes the world go round."*

Even religious texts are quoted, including:

- *"It is easier for a camel to pass through the eye of a needle than for a rich man to enter the Kingdom of Heaven."*

While it may well be true that these "sound-bite" pieces of advice were sound when first formulated, most (although, not all) are less than helpful in the modern Western world. This is especially true, if you harbour any ambition to accumulate real wealth.

In my opinion, one of the greatest obstacles to real wealth creation is ourselves! It is what we think we know about money that often acts as a barrier to accumulating more. This book, along with my first one (*The Tricks of the Rich*, also published by Oak Tree Press), is an attempt on my part to convince the reader to discard most of what you think you know and to replace it with genuine "financial intelligence". As you read this, I hope that you will learn that:

♦ Investing money is far easier when you have the knowledge.

♦ Risks are nowhere near as dangerous as you perceive them to be.

♦ For the most part, the successful accumulation of wealth has much more to do with the "how" you do it, than "what" investments you actually make.

If you are happy with the wealth accumulation that is going on in your life; if you are happy that the financial decisions of your past have always been the right ones; if you are happy with the amount of tax you pay; then you probably have no need to read this book. However, before you do read it, if you are less than happy with your financial world, recognise that something is going to have to change. Change itself is difficult and most people I know would do almost anything to avoid it, but only change will alter your results. Albert Einstein had a definition of madness:

> "Doing the same thing over and over again and expecting a different result."

If you are to change the results of your financial world, then you are going to have to do things differently and, in my view, this type of change can only occur if you are willing to change yourself!

I am reminded of a conversation with a close personal friend quite recently who asked me "why" I was writing these financial books. *"I want the reader to understand"*, I said, *"that much of what they think they know about money is not actually correct. For example"*, I continued, *"you know the old phrase 'Money is the root of all evil'. Well, I am amazed at how often I hear that repeated and there can be no doubt that people who do repeat it allow it to affect their financial actions. There are many, many examples of such phrases and all, to a greater or lesser extent, must affect the financial decision-making of those who quote them."*

Some of the "many, many examples" are listed above, others you can come up with yourself, and if you have lived your life by these mantras and you are happy with your financial results, then you need change nothing. But please recognise that, if you are not happy, then it is at least possible that these mantras are wrong.

Consider the following: if it is always correct to follow the mantra "don't put all your eggs in one basket", why then are some of the world's richest people those that did just that – for example, Bill Gates of Microsoft, Steve Jobs of Apple, Richard Branson of Virgin? While it is true that these people have "diversified" since they became wealthy, the simple reality is that they got there in the first place because "they had all their eggs in one basket".

If it is always correct to "neither a borrower or a lender be", why then are most of the world's richest businesses involved in "lending money" and show me, if you can (and other than those lucky enough to win great wealth, you'll find it a difficult task), a wealthy person who has not "borrowed" money.

I could go on and on, but let us leave it there. Just know that if you have not successfully created real, sustainable, wealth up until now, the financial mantras of the past are most likely to be part of the problem and not part of the solution.

FINANCIAL INTELLIGENCE

I have worked in the financial services industry, since I left formal education in 1980 and yet, in truth, I have only truly understood how wealth is created for the last few years.

My first book was an attempt on my part to give the reader the basics of "financial intelligence". When I use the term "intelligence", I do not mean "cleverness". Instead, I use it as it is used in Central Intelligence Agency, in that it refers to information. In truth, to make any financial decision to your best advantage you need to be in possession of three vital pieces of information:

- ◆ The costs.
- ◆ The benefits.
and
- ◆ The risks.

I have never said this to anyone who has disagreed with me – we all recognise the simple truth of it. If we are denied one of these vital pieces of information, and yet make a decision, whether or not that decision proves profitable is in the lap of the gods – we may benefit or we may not. None of us, I imagine, would buy a second-hand car at a knock-down price without having it checked out by a qualified mechanic. We know, instinctively it might seem, but in reality we have learned by our own (or others') mistakes, to be suspicious of a knock-down price, realising that the relative cost is likely to have a logical explanation. The car may have been crashed, stolen, or may not be exactly as it seems. These are the most likely explanations, more likely by far than simply assuming we are lucky or have come across the bargain of the century. The point of this is that we have learned, we have gained invaluable experience that allows us to protect ourselves and our money from a bad decision.

Unfortunately, the other point I wish to make is that we have not learned about money itself. We go through years and years of formal education but yet the vast bulk of us – and I include myself here – leave that education knowing nothing about money. We have no idea how to invest it, no idea of how we should earn it, no idea of how we should leave it to our children when we eventually "shuffle off this mortal coil". This lack of personal knowledge means that we have to seek advice and, even then, our lack of knowledge may mean we choose the wrong "adviser".

Those of you who have read *The Tricks of the Rich* will know I favour having a financial goal, around which you make your financial decisions. I describe the goal as the achievement of "financial freedom":

> *"Getting to a stage where your investment assets can replace your income without the necessity for you to continue working".*

The reason I favour such a focus, quite simply, is that it makes your financial decisions easier. In my experience, most people make financial decisions on an *ad hoc* basis and more with their hearts than their heads. This means that our emotions are in charge of our decision-making process and the two feelings to the fore are fear and greed. The former is a paralysing emotion (as it is for most creatures on this planet) and means we do not take action. The latter motivates us and, in many cases, blinds us to the true facts (costs, benefits and risks). Making your decisions with a financial freedom focus means that, in the future, you will make your financial decisions with one key question to the fore:

> *"Does this bring me closer to, or move me further away from, my financial target?"*

As we go through life, we make millions of financial decisions; those that have the potential to create wealth are decisions that may bring us "closer to" our financial target. Those that simply consume our income, without any wealth accumulation potential, will move us "further away" from our goals.

One of the most important lessons I learned, as I started to concentrate on creating my own wealth, was that, when making a "further away" decision (like the purchase of a car, a new kitchen, a larger, flatter TV, etc), there is a considerable opportunity cost – which is one of the costs very few of us take into our decision-making process! Most people make these decisions on a *"Can I afford it?"* basis and a huge percentage of such purchases are funded by way of short-term debt. Therefore, in many cases, the decision is made based on a *"Can I afford the monthly repayments?"* basis. Let us look at an example of buying a motor car to demonstrate what I mean.

If you decided today to buy a €50,000 motor car on a purchase lease charging 9% *p.a.* interest, the monthly repayments would be in the region of €1,070 over five years, or a total of €64,200. Here is where buyers make the first mistake. If I asked you what you paid for the car, you would say *"€50,000"* – but, of course, the true cost was 28.4% more! Now, remember that you had to earn considerably more than €1,070 per month to repay this amount and, assuming the top tax cost of 46% (41% tax and 5% levies), this means that the true cost was €1,981.48 per month of your gross (pre-tax) income. This, from an earnings point of view, means that the car has cost you €118,888.80 or 138% more than the price on the windscreen. This gross amount is relevant since, as you will see later, you could have invested the €1,981.48 per month instead and, if you received a 6% *p.a.* growth in the investment, your accumulated wealth at the end of five years would be €138,989. So your new car didn't cost you €50,000 – it cost you €138,989!

Accumulating wealth, as could be said of any field of endeavour you care to mention, takes attention to detail and, in the example above, we are attending to detail. Most purchasers of the car in this example would tell you it cost them €50,000, but they were not truly aware of the real costs (one of the three vital pieces of information that lead to good financial decision-making). They made their decision based on *"Can I afford the monthly repayments?"* and, in the process, robbed themselves of €138,989 of real wealth!

For future reference, should you have such a decision to make, please note that I have taken no account of the road tax, running costs or the depreciation of value – all genuine costs that should be considered. If I did include these, I imagine the true cost of the car in question would be close to four times more than the price on the windscreen.

My first book, which dealt with this consumer debt issue in far greater detail, and which I recommend you read if you have not already, was written to give the reader the basics of true financial intelligence. This book is designed to give you much more detail on the processes and structures you can use to create as much wealth as is possible in your circumstances. Far too often, in my view, those of us who try to create a little wealth do so in ways that frustrate our efforts. Our inability to identify the costs, the risks and the benefits of any financial action is one frustration; the lack of knowledge in how to structure our financial affairs is another. My first book attempted to give the reader the knowledge to assist with the former, this one attempts to do the same for the latter.

This is the second book that I have produced on what some say is most people's favourite subject – money. Whether it is, or even should be, most people's "favourite" isn't important. What is undeniably true is that money is an integral and vital element in our daily lives.

FINANCIAL FREEDOM

I remember a heated discussion a number of years ago with my wife, fuelled as it inevitably was back then by my long working hours and short, less than frequent, holidays. I was explaining that, if she wanted, we could sell all our assets (and pay off our liabilities), buy a house in the country and live a frugal (but who is to say less happy?) life. If she was prepared to live without the luxuries that my long hours and infrequent holidays allowed us to enjoy, she could have me by her side 24/7.

"You always bring things back to money" came her less than happy reply. *"Life is about more than money."*

"Of course it is", I agreed. *"But the life we lead is only made possible by the money we earn, whether we like it or not. We are in a lucky position, that we have a genuine choice. We could sell up, move home, live more frugally and we could live for the rest of our lives without having to earn another penny. However, we cannot live our current life without my having to invest the time and effort to build a business (and an investment portfolio) that can produce the income we need and which will eventually produce that income without me having to work at all!"*

I cannot remember whether my argument immediately swayed Jenny's opinion; it's most likely it was met by *"You have an answer to everything."* However, she eventually saw the point. Luckily, since then I have managed to have more free time and I put in far less hours than I used to and I am still working towards the time when our investments can recreate our income without the necessity for me to work.

I have a real financial target and I am working towards achieving it inside a real (and specific) timeframe and, to me, this is very much part of *"it ain't necessarily what you do; it's the way that you do it"*.

You see, in my opinion, most people (and I mean the vast majority of people in the Western world) never achieve their financial ambitions because, quite frankly, they have no real ambitions at all. If you asked 100 people, 1,000 people, 100,000 people what their financial ambition is, to a man (or woman) they would reply with something like *"I want to be rich"*. However, *"I want to be rich"* is far too vague, there is no specific amount, which invariably means that there is no plan and no action being taken to achieve the goal.

The real problem with *"I want to be rich"* is that *"rich"* is relative. I heard an American comedian discussing this subject recently (obviously in a different context), who made the same point: *"Rich is relative. If Bill Gates woke up tomorrow morning with my money, he'd probably throw himself out the nearest window."* Now, this well-known comic is, by any definition, a rich man but his point is well-made. The judgement of "rich" depends on where you view it from. To many, the comedian is a rich man but, to many more, including Bill Gates, he is a relative pauper. So "rich" means different things to different people and this is why, in my opinion, it is useless as a financial ambition.

Of course, I did not always think this way. In my early career, I was that *"I want to be rich"* individual and, like so many others, I did relatively little about achieving my goal. In hindsight, I believe there were two main reasons for my inaction. First, I did not really have a financial goal; second, I was ignorant of the ways in which wealth is created.

More recently, having established my financial advisory business, *Financial Engineering Network Ltd.*, with two very clever and hard-working partners, I managed to clarify my thinking on the goal. Today, I am working towards what we call "financial freedom", which we define as:

> *"Getting to a stage where your investment assets can replace your income without the necessity for you to continue working".*

The idea of managing one's money towards a clearly-defined financial target is discussed at length in my previous book (*The*

Tricks of the Rich) and I strongly suggest that you read it before you read this one. It was written to allow the reader to learn (and if reader feedback is anything to go by, it has achieved its objective), for the very first time, how money actually works, how to use the financial institutions to your best advantage and how to really plan your journey to your financial freedom.

This book has been written to delve that bit deeper into the structures of wealth creation, maintenance and retention and, for some, may make little sense without having read, and acted upon, the suggestions in *The Tricks of the Rich*, which comes with a basic CD-Rom that allows you to calculate your own target and to put right some of the typical errors we all make when investing, borrowing, repaying or spending our money.

And, finally, a *caveat*: Throughout this book, I give numerical examples and, for the most part, I round these numbers up or down to the nearest €5. Also, where tax calculations are concerned, while every effort has been made to ensure that the tax rates and regulations illustrated are correct on the date of publication, readers need to be aware that tax rates and regulations change constantly – another reason to seek out professional assistance when you come to apply these tactics to your own financial world.

1
CHOOSE THE RIGHT ADVISER

As mentioned in the **Introduction**, the fact that most of us enter our working lives with little or no knowledge of money means we are dependent upon getting advice from others. Although I am a firm believer in learning as much about money as you can (hence, I have produced two books on the subject), I am also a realist and so I recognise that, to implement some of the structures that are described here, you will require outside assistance. Thus, one of the first processes you may have to go through is choosing an adviser.

Even if you know everything there is to know about wealth creation, an adviser may prove useful. In my own advisory firm, when meeting a potential client for the first time, I sometimes say: *"It is a 24-hour-a-day job to earn the money you earn and to have a life. It is also a 24-hour-a-day job to manage your money to achieve financial freedom and to have a life. Even if you know all that I know, where will you find the time to do the second job?"*

The typical answer is probably the one you are thinking of right now: *"I will not be able to."*

So, as I often say to potential clients who give me this answer: *"I am applying for the second job"*.

So, how do you pick the right adviser? The first thing to do is to get a list of all fee-based advisers in your area. This list should be available from the Financial Regulator[1] or from the adviser representative bodies[2].

AVOID "FREE" ADVICE

But, I hear you ask: *"Why do I need to pay a fee? Isn't free advice available?"*

Yes, there is much available that purports to be "free advice", but it is **not** advice! If you are getting "free" advice, then either you are getting that advice from a charitable institution or it is "free" because someone else is paying the adviser. I am unaware of any institution in the wealth creation arena that operates in a charitable fashion and, therefore, if you are getting (or seek out in the future) "free" advice, then it is probably because someone else is paying.

---

[1]   In Ireland, the Financial Regulator (PO Box 9138, College Green, Dublin 2 – phone: 01 410 4000 – email: consumerinfo@financialregulator.ie – web: www.financialregulator.ie).

[2]   In Ireland, for example, the Irish Brokers Association (87 Merrion Square, Dublin 2 – phone: 01 661 3067 – email: info@irishbrokers.ie – web: www.iba.ie) or the Institute of Chartered Accountants in Ireland (CA House, 83 Pembroke Road, Dublin 4 – phone: 01 637 7200 – email: ca@icai.ie – web: www.icai.ie).

I am reminded of a radio advertisement that I heard recently for a computer service and repair company that starts like this:

"Free, free, free – that's exactly what good advice should cost ..."

... and goes on to tell the listeners that a representative will call, give the consumer's computer a complete health-check and tell them what is wrong and how much it will cost to fix. When I first heard this ad, my reaction was: *"What rubbish! They will always find something wrong and will want to sell me some service or software package, otherwise they make nothing!"*

After all, the repair company is not a charity and is surely trying to make money (if not, it will be out of business by the time you read this).

I imagine many readers would have the same reaction as I did. If so, why would you not have exactly the same reaction when offered "free" financial advice?

For some reason, the selling of financial products and services, for most of us, is not considered selling at all – but, of course, it is! People paid a commission to sell us something, whether it is clothes, computer repairs or financial products, are salespeople, they are not advisers – no matter what their business card says. Thus, no more than one shopkeeper will tell you that you can buy a better product at a lower price in a competitor's shop, neither will a bank salesperson tell you about a competitor bank's product, even if the competing product is better.

I refer to this kind of commission-remunerated advice as **biased**. No matter what your financial circumstances or requirements, salespeople will always try to sell you something – otherwise, they will not get paid. If you are attempting to create wealth, biased advice is to be avoided, whether it's provided by a financial institution or by an independent agent,[3] who is paid commission by the financial institutions.

AVOID ISOLATED ADVICE

From the list of fee-based financial advisers, you need to identify one who can deal with all aspects of your finances.

I do not mean that this person must do everything for you, but they must be able to consider your entire financial situation when giving advice. Otherwise, you may suffer the inefficiencies that isolated advice can cause. Your new adviser needs to prove to you that he/she has the knowledge to take any and all of the following into account as his/her advice is formulated:

- ◆ Tax (both corporate and personal, covering income and capital taxes).
- ◆ Investments (both on-shore and off-shore).
- ◆ Risk evaluation.
- ◆ Mortgages and other loans (personal and corporate).
- ◆ Retirement schemes (both private and "off-the-shelf" versions).
- ◆ Pensions.
- ◆ Life and health (all types) insurance.
- ◆ Legal issues.
- ◆ Succession planning and wills.
- ◆ Property (residential, commercial and retail).

In my view, your new adviser needs to be able to discuss each of these areas with some degree of expertise, simply because each

---

3   In financial services, an "independent" agent is a person who is not directly employed by a financial institution but whose income, much more often than not, is based on commissions received from one or more financial institutions for the sale of their products. An agent who is directly employed by a financial institution, or who deals only with a single institution, is described as a "tied" agent.

of these areas has the potential to either increase or decrease your wealth. I know it may be difficult to find one person with such breadth of knowledge and experience; however, it should be easier to find a firm that will satisfy your requirements. So, in looking for an adviser, you should probably be looking for a firm of advisers, and thus you could discount any one-man-bands on the list, unless he/she has some affiliation with a larger firm that can provide this broader expertise.

I am adamant that you need this full range of expertise because I have so often witnessed how isolated advice can be detrimental to the creation of wealth. I am sure that many of you will have heard the old saying that my grandmother quoted nearly every day of her life:

> *"Look after the pennies and the pounds will look after themselves."*

The problems caused by isolated advice generally affect the "pennies" and, in my experience, many people ignore them because of the relatively small amounts involved. But these small amounts accumulate – and can cost you big-time!

Let's view it another way. Your attempt to create financial freedom can be likened to an attempt to fill a barrel with water. The barrel has a few small leaks, but you are able to get water in much more quickly than it leaks out, and thus you succeed in filling the barrel to the brim – and you achieve your goal. However, reaching the goal is only one part of the task; once you reach it, you want to maintain it. If you do not fix the leaks, then your water, however slowly, will drain away.

If you do not fix the leaks, however small, in your financial world, eventually your assets will drain away. Also, I find that the very act of fixing the "small stuff" in our financial world is extremely educational and means that such inefficiencies are unlikely ever to creep into your world again.

Let me give you an example of the type of financial inefficiencies that isolationist advice can lead to.

I imagine I am safe in assuming that no reader would be foolish enough to walk into a bank and borrow money at a rate of 9% *p.a.*, and then cross the foyer and put the borrowed money on deposit at 3% *p.a.* However, if my clients in *Financial Engineering Network Ltd.* are typical of the population in general, at least half the people reading this book do just exactly that.

You see, if you separate these two transactions by time and institution – you make the two decisions at different times and with different advisers (or salespeople perhaps?) – so that you borrow money to buy a car on one date and, several months later, when a bonus comes your way, you tuck it away in a deposit account "for a rainy day", the effect is the same: you are paying a higher interest rate on your borrowings than you are receiving on your savings, and you are borrowing your own money and paying for the privilege!

Now, I understand how so many people make this mistake; not every financial decision is part of an integrated plan and time dulls the memory. We make financial decisions on the run, grabbing moments here and there to think about, and take action with, our own money and rarely, if ever, does our last (or second last, or third last …) financial decision impact on the one we are making right now.

However, if you have a good financial adviser in your corner, who knows your financial circumstances inside and out, who has the experience and expertise to help in all areas of your financial life, then these mistakes will not be made and financial inefficiencies will not erode your "pennies".

Other inefficiencies that could be keeping you from truly starting to generate real wealth include:

- ♦ Failing to take advantage of all tax concessions.
- ♦ Earning your income in an inefficient manner.
- ♦ Misunderstanding risk and reward.

♦ Taking financial advice from those paid commission to sell you "stuff".

♦ Investing only in what you know, without making any attempt to expand your own knowledge.

♦ Accepting loan offers that are structured to the lender's best advantage, rather than your own.

♦ Making offshore investments without fully investigating (and thus understanding) all the tax implications.

♦ Avoiding the world's stock markets because you fear them.

♦ Over-accumulating assets in your own name and, by so doing, substantially increasing the taxes to be paid by your heirs.

♦ Borrowing for consumables.

♦ Not borrowing for investments.

♦ Failing to make a will and thus leaving the distribution of your assets to the State.

The list of potential inefficiencies could go on and on, but I will not labour the point any more. There is one more item I will add, however:

♦ Failing to make, and to re-visit, a plan.

MAKE A PLAN

When choosing your financial adviser for the future, you already know that he/she must be fee-based and must demonstrate an ability to add value in all areas of your financial life. Whatever the original size of your list of prospective advisers, by omitting those who do not meet these two criteria, I imagine it is now quite a short list. I suggest it is time to go meet those remaining.

The first thing that I personally would insist upon is that any adviser worthy of consideration must mention a **plan** and explain how they would work with you to achieve that plan.

The main reason for writing this book is to demonstrate to the reader that creating real wealth is as much about the "how's" (**how** you act with, and around, your money), as it is about the 'what's' (**what** type of investments you use). The first "how" is **how** to choose the right adviser. Working to a plan allows both you and the adviser judge progress easily, simply by asking yourself regularly: *"How are we doing towards our goals?"*

Your first meeting with each of your short-listed advisers should cost you little or nothing. As an adviser, I always offer the first consultation for free. After all, I do not know whether I can help someone until I meet with them and hear a little about them. If I do not yet know whether I can help, the potential client will not know either and, in such an engagement, I cannot justify a fee.

At this first meeting, expect the adviser to give you a broad history of his/her business and details of the expertise of the firm's staff. Expect him/her to ask some probing questions (without yet seeking in-depth and private information), to get a broad picture of your current financial circumstances. Then you should be told what it is the adviser believes he/she can do for you and how much you can expect to pay for the first phase. You should not make a knee-jerk decision on the spot, and if the adviser is pushing for an immediate decision, personally I would walk away and cross him/her off my list.

What you should do is:

♦ Ask for all details discussed at your initial meeting to be confirmed in writing and on the headed paper of the adviser.

♦ Ask for a copy of the firm's fee schedule and their terms and conditions of business.

♦ Ask for client testimonials from people who have already dealt with the adviser, including, if possible, one you can get verbally by contacting the person directly.

♦ Tell the adviser when he/she can expect you to make your decision on whether to engage their services. In my opinion, the adviser should be aware you are shopping around.

Once you have visited all of the advisers on your short-list and have gathered the relevant information, you are in a position to make your final decision. If my experience is anything to go by, there is likely to be one adviser who stands head-and-shoulders above the rest, so, if you go through the process described, your adviser likely will have picked himself/herself.

2
IDENTIFY THE REAL COSTS OF "OFF-THE-SHELF" INVESTMENT PRODUCTS

The marketplace is awash with investment projects and products vying for your money – indeed, it seems there is a never-ending supply. Ignoring, for the moment at least, the type of investments on offer (which generally fall into one of four categories: equity (stocks and shares), property, gilts (Government and corporate loan paper) and cash), I want to first demonstrate for you how to identify the true costs of these projects and products.

MIS-ALIGNED GOALS

I used to work for some of the financial institutions who manufacture and market such "off-the-shelf" products and it is their, what I like to call, "I'm alright Jack" approach to product design that makes me wary of them. Invariably, many of the charges levied within these products are taken immediately and the ongoing charges (which, as you will see later, can be huge) are levied whether or not the product actually makes you money. Thus, from the product manufacturer's point of view, and from the salesman's point of view too (as they get paid up-front), the future success of the product is of much less importance than it is for you, the investor. What we have, therefore, is a complete misalignment of goals because the future success of the underlying investment is of paramount importance to you. When such a misalignment of goals exists, it tends to lead to one party being served better than the other.

We have all witnessed the massive value uplifts enjoyed by our financial institutions over the last couple of decades (in my last book, I was able to show how *Bank of Ireland*'s value has grown by circa 18% *p.a.* over 20 years[4]), although I imagine very few of their clients have enjoyed the same type of growth. As I said earlier, with a misalignment of goals someone gets the bad end of the stick. We all know this to be true, whether one is referring to an adviser/advisee relationship, a business partnership or even, dare I say it, a romantic relationship. When two agendas are at work, one usurps the other. When two people have different objectives, one always wins out and one, relatively speaking, loses. Unfortunately, from a wealth accumulation perspective, I think there is no doubt that the parties to these relationships getting far richer are the institutions, despite the fact that they purport to be in business to make their clients richer.

---

[4]   Figures sourced from Brian Carey, 'Home truths are needed from the horse's mouth', *The Sunday Times*, 9 October 2005.

As mentioned in the **Introduction,** one of the key pieces of information you need when making any investment decision is the costs. One of the major problems for any potential investor in these "manufactured" products is that while, under legislation, the costs must be outlined to you, they are generally illustrated in such a way that they look far less than they actually are. By way of an example, let us look at the "real" costs of investing in a standard personal retirement savings account (PRSA). I have chosen a standard PRSA as its cost has been dictated by legislation and, certainly where regular contribution savings products are concerned, therefore it is likely to be one of the cheapest 'manufactured' products on the market.

Assume the following:

♦ You invest €100 per month into a standard PRSA for a period of 20 years.

♦ The monthly contribution remains level throughout the investment period.

♦ The gross return (before charges) on the underlying fund will be 6% *p.a.*

The first of the two charges the institution is allowed (under legislation) to levy on you is a 5% bid/offer spread, which is generally shown as the difference between the buying and selling price of a "unit" in the investment fund. This means it is levied on each of your €100 monthly investments (the day you make the investment, its value drops to €95, since you lose 5% in charges). Over 20 years, the overall cost of this charge is **€1,200** (€100 x 12 x 20 x 0.05).

The second charge that the institution is permitted to levy is an annual management fee. Within a standard PRSA, that is 1% *p.a.* However, unlike the bid/offer spread, this charge is levied on the total of the investment fund (not on what you pay in) each year and its true cost is far more difficult to calculate. As the manufacturers and sellers are allowed to quote it in percentage terms, I am sure many investors assume this 1% levy costs just one-fifth of the similarly quoted 5% bid/offer spread; however, they are mistaken. The effect of a 1% annual management fee is to reduce the effective gross return to the investor from 6% before charges, in this example, to 5%. By calculating the return on the investment at both the 6% assumed gross return and at the 5% after charges return, we can see the "real" cost of this charge.

Estimated value of fund after 20 years	€
@ 6% *pa* return	46,435
@ 5% *pa* return	41,275
Difference = Cost to the investor	**5,160**

Note: All figures rounded up or down to nearest €5.

So the cost to you of the 1% annual management fee charged over the 20 years is **€5,160** – equivalent to 21.5% of your total investment of €24,000 (€100 x 12 x 20). Some might argue that this is an unfair (unfair to the financial institutions, I suspect) way of illustrating cost, arguing that the 1% levy is on the overall fund, which grows to an estimated final value of €41,275 in our example, and that €5,160 is only 12.5% of €41,275. However, I do not contribute to this school of thought as, in my opinion, it is the money we invest that must be used to judge value for money. The only fair way (to you, the investor) to illustrate costs is by comparing them to the money you part with.

You can see now that, even when costs are minimised by government intervention, in our example, the product manufacturer takes a total of 26.5% of the money we invest in a standard PRSA.

If we run the same assumptions for a 10-year investment, the overall costs drop to 12.31% of the investment. Over 30 years, the costs increase to 53.28%.

If you have already invested in a standard PRSA, might you have made a different decision had you known the true costs? I imagine you would have, which (I'm searching for a silver lining here) in itself is proof that superior knowledge leads to better financial decision-making.

Manufactured products have substantial associated costs. Since neither the manufacturers nor their sales agents will identify those charges clearly for you, you need to be able to calculate them for yourself. **Appendix 1** is a table that allows you identify the true cost of the annual management fee, the most complicated of the costs to calculate. The next time you are considering an "off-the-shelf" investment, make sure you ask for the annual management fee and use this table to identify the real cost.

Note that I am not for a moment saying that the lower the annual management fee, the better – that would be far too simplistic. However, you now know that, for a higher fee, you need to be convinced that the underlying investment is likely to perform considerably better than a low-cost alternative.

This leads me neatly into the first question you need to ask about the investment fund:

> *"What has been the performance of the investment fund over the last 5 to 10 years, net of all charges?"*

You are **not** looking for a quotation here. After all, within legislative guidelines, the manufacturer or agent can estimate any number they like for the future performance of the fund. What you want is a real-life example of someone who had invested in, and withdrawn from, the fund in the past.

Neither are you interested in performance league tables like the ones that appear in the press from time to time. Many product sales people arm themselves with such tables (I know this, because I used to do it myself) and use them to demonstrate the historical performance of the investment fund they are selling. Not only are such league tables useless, but they can be completely misleading, since they generally quote gross returns (before charges), which means that no investor in the funds has actually received the annual yields being reported. Not only this, but there is potential for what appears to be the best performer to be the worst, if the charges within the particular fund exceeds the out-performance being illustrated.

By insisting that you see real figures from a real investment, all of the charges that are levied in the fund will be reflected. If you are denied this information, I think it is safe to assume that the performance history is poor and that the fund is likely to be best avoided.

There will be times, of course, when you are offered a new fund, one without any history. In such circumstances, you need to ask a number of key questions so that you can make a properly-informed decision and I will deal with these questions later in this chapter. For now, I want to concentrate on charges.

CHARGES

In addition to the bid/offer spread and the annual management fee, you may have to contend with:

♦ Commission.

♦ Non-allocation periods.

♦ Policy fees.

♦ Allocation rates.

I have dealt with each charge under a separate heading below, giving a broad description of the charge itself and some ideas on how you might "haggle" your way to improved terms and conditions. But, first, let's deal with the two charges we have already identified.

Bid / offer Spread

This charge tends to be uniform throughout the marketplace, levied at 5% of the investment amount (or of the regular payment). It can be reduced through what the industry describes as "extra allocation". You should always ask whether an extra allocation can be made available to you, especially if your investment is significant. Also, a sales agent, who transacts substantial business with the product manufacturer, should have some commercial "pull" with the manufacturer and may be convinced to use it on your behalf to win your business.

For the purpose of illustration, let's look at two examples:

♦ First, where you are investing a lump sum of €50,000.

♦ Second, where your investment is €200 per month.

Assuming you pay the full 5% bid / offer cost and receive a net 5% *p.a.* return on your investment, the following are the estimated values of your investment over various terms:

Term (years)	Estimated Value of Lump Sum Investment €	Estimated Value of Regular Payment Investment €
5	60,625	12,975
10	77,370	29,625
15	98,750	50.995
20	126,030	78,420
25	160,850	113,620
30	205,290	158,790

Note: All figures rounded up/down to nearest €5.

Now, let's assume that you negotiate an extra allocation of 2%, which will mean that 102% of your investment amount is allocated to the fund. The estimates illustrated in the previous table increase as follows:

Term (years)	Estimated Value of Lump Sum Investment €	Estimated Value of Regular Payment Investment €
5	61,835	13,235
10	78,920	30,220
15	100,725	52,015
20	128,550	79,990
25	164,070	115,890
30	209,400	161,965

Note: All figures rounded up/down to nearest €5.

So, by negotiating an extra allocation of 2% at the beginning, your wealth increases by the same 2% in the future.

Now, let's also assume that, at the time you negotiate the extra allocation, you also pay attention to the annual management fee. If you reduce that fee by 0.25%, for example (typically, only possible by going for a lower cost alternate product (see next section)), the following will be the future estimates:

Term (years)	Estimated Value of Lump Sum Investment €	Estimated Value of Regular Payment Investment €
5	62,575	13,320
10	80,820	30,635
15	104,380	53,130
20	134,815	82,360
25	174,120	120,340
30	224,885	169,695

Note: All figures rounded up/down to nearest €5.

By negotiating a reduction in both charges **together**, your estimated future wealth accumulation increases, depending on the time period, by between 3.22% and 9.55% for lump sums and between 2.66% and 6.87% for regular payments. How well you negotiate, as you invest into this type of product, influences the wealth you will create.

Annual Management Fee

By asking the relevant question, you will know the annual management fee of the investment product you are considering and you can use the table in **Appendix 1** to calculate its real cost. Typically, funds are administered in such a way that means it is not possible for you to "haggle" away part of this cost (but it's always worth trying!).

However, you now realise the huge impact that this charge will have on the future success of your investment and, thus, you need to be convinced that you will reap higher benefits by paying a greater fee. If you cannot negotiate a reduction in the annual management fee on the investment product you are considering, ask about alternate funds that invest in the same underlying investment and compare the gross returns (here the league tables do come in handy). Convince yourself (or not, as the case might be) that the fund management company asking for the higher fee is delivering a return greater than the additional cost; if it is not, use the lower cost alternative.

Commission

Whether employed directly by the financial institution or a self-employed person paid by the financial institution, the sales agent is being paid to sell you the product. The level of commission payable to the selling agent is very much dependent upon the type of product you are being sold and the relationship between the salesperson and the financial institution that has manufactured the product. Rates can be as low as 0% (where the agent charges a fee and chooses a nil-commission product on your behalf) and as high as 90% of the first year's contribution (which applies to most life (death) insurance policies). The first question you need to ask the selling agent is what commission levels are being paid.

Once you are made aware of the commission involved (and, if the selling agent will not tell you, I think you should end your discussions immediately), you are in a position to judge value for money. Asking how the selling agent can justify the payments is vital: what he or she is doing for **you** should be your only interest.

One of the main problems I have with commission is that the level of payment to the selling agent is linked to the amount you invest. So, for example, looking at a standard lump sum investment product paying a commission of 3%, if you invest €10,000, the selling agent receives €300 but, if you invest €100,000, he/she receives €3,000. It is hard to see how any selling agent can justify such a massive increase in their income – after all, the job they do is likely to be much the same no matter how much or how little you invest. They may review the "off-the-shelf" marketplace, meet with you to discuss your requirements and then recommend a product. It is only right and proper that they are remunerated for their efforts, but in our example, would you knowingly pay 10 times more?

Once you know the commission payable, you should also know that most off-the-shelf products have a choice of commission rates to the seller. You are not, and I stress this part, **not** looking for a rebate of commission. Not only should a rebate be declared to the Revenue as "income" (and even if you do not do this, which would be unadvisable, the selling agent may make a third-party Return; after all, if they do not, they pay tax on income they no longer keep) but, if there are tax breaks associated with the product (such as a pension), a rebate could place those tax breaks in jeopardy. What you are looking for is a fair price and your agent should enter into negotiations with you. It is true that "haggling" in this fashion is not easy; you need to develop a "hard neck", but it will be productive and, like most things, the more you do it, the easier it becomes.

Decide yourself what you believe to be a fair price for the agent's time and expertise and ask if he/she is willing to do the job for that price. Then, once an agreement is reached on a figure, ask the agent to confirm it in writing, expressing the agreed charge in both euro and percentage terms, as well as confirming how he/she will receive it from the product manufacturer. Finally, the same letter should confirm the arrangement as a better deal when compared to standard terms and should tell you how these improved terms are reflected within the product you have bought.

Non-allocation Periods

This charging structure has become less and less common over the last few years but there are still products using it. Typically, it applies to regular contribution investment products and it does "exactly what it says on the tin". For a period of time, **none** of the money you invest is actually invested.

In my opinion, such a charging method is to be avoided if at all possible, as the immediate and obvious cost is really only half the story. In any regular contribution investment, it is the money invested early that has the potential to make you the most profit (it is the amount invested longest) and so this charging method can actually cost you money for the duration of your investment. Knowing that it exists allows you to ask whether this particular charge applies to the product being offered; finding out that it does allows you to ask whether an alternative charging structure is available, or allows you to haggle.

Typically, this charge is expressed on a time basis (for example, no allocation for the first six months); realising that this is the case means you can ask for that non-allocation period to be shortened.

Allocation Rates

The allocation rate of any investment product is expressed as a percentage of the amount you invest (either lump sum or regular contributions). Thus, for example, an allocation rate of 98.5% means that only 98.5% of your investment amount reaches the investment fund.

Once again, possessing this knowledge allows you to ask the selling agent for the allocation rate; having the question answered starts the haggling process. Do not be afraid, especially when you are investing a large amount, to seek the highest allocation rate possible and bear in mind that the rate can be higher than 100%. The simple fact, from the seller's and financial institution's point of view, is that "half a loaf is better than no loaf at all" and I have seen allocation rates as high as 107%. It pays to know what rate you are being offered and it goes without saying (but I am going to say it anyway) that the more of your money that reaches the investment fund, the greater the wealth you will create in the long term.

I do not want to give you the impression that all the costs and charges outlined here are present in all off-the-shelf products; they are not. However, such products will have one or more of these costs and, therefore, you need to ask about each, if only to confirm that the charge does not apply. Once you are aware of all the costs, you are in a position to negotiate reductions, a position that you may not have been in heretofore.

OTHER QUESTIONS YOU SHOULD ASK

I mentioned earlier that I would give you some questions to ask about off-the-shelf investments, the answers to which will improve your knowledge (of costs, benefits and risks) and thus lead to better decision-making. You need to ask these questions in addition to the historical performance question on page **25**. Here they are:

♦ **Have the people managing the fund changed in the last while?** It is people who manage money, not financial institutions. If the fund has a good historical performance, then you want to be sure that those who produced the good returns are there still, managing your money. If they are not, then ask where have they gone (usually, they will have moved to another fund management role with another company), as it may be prudent to follow them with your money.

♦ **Has the size (the total amount invested) of the fund altered dramatically over the period for which you have been given the historical performance data?** It is common for smaller investment funds to outperform their larger competitors. This is because a smaller fund can change tack much more readily than a larger counterpart and thus, for example, can take more advantage of a "good run" on a particular share. Consider it this way: for a fund with an overall value of just €1m to put 20% of its value into a "hot stock", the fund manager need only get his/her hands on €200,000 of the stock; for a fund worth €100m to do the same, €20m of the stock has to be found, a much more difficult task. Likewise, if a particular element of the fund is performing badly, it is far easier for the small fund manager to take corrective action than for his larger counterpart. By asking this question, you can gauge whether much of the historical performance was delivered by the size of the fund and, if it has grown substantially,

you will know that its increased size may mean that the
past performance cannot be repeated.

♦ **How do you know that the year-on-year performance the
fund manager tells you about is actually the performance
of the underlying investments?** In Ireland, most
institutionally-manufactured investment products are not
independently audited and thus you have to take the fund
manager's word on annual returns. Maybe it is the cynic in
me, but I am uncomfortable with such a system, as I
believe that, unfortunately, given an opportunity to "put
their best foot forward", most people will do so. It is, of
course, your money and the choice is yours alone but, if
you know there is no independent auditing, that
knowledge may change your final decision.

♦ **What will happen to your money if the fund manager
(either institution or specialist intermediary) goes into
liquidation before the investment matures?** Believe it or
not, many off-the-shelf investment products in Ireland are
actually owned by the institution or intermediary and,
thus, when you invest your money, you have actually
transferred it to their ownership. The policy document (or
unit certificate, perhaps) you get in return is effectively an
IOU. In such circumstances, if the institution goes bust
before the end of the investment term, you will be lined up
in the street with the people who sold them their
computers, phone systems, etc, wondering how many
cents in the euro you are going to get from the liquidator.
Being aware of the legal structure of any investment may
well change your final decision.

♦ **When can I get my money back?** Many investment
products allow immediate and ongoing access to your
investment amount, while many others (sometimes due to
legislation – for example, pensions) have strict rules on
how and when you can get your money back. Syndicated

investment funds (usually invested in property) can require a majority of the investors to want their money back before you can exit, or even can be constituted in such a way as to give the promoters a say over when the investment comes to an end. The problem here is that it is unlikely that all of the investors in such a project (or the promoters) will have the same agenda as you. They may have a longer or shorter timeframe in mind, which could lead to your money being stuck inside a product, or released from it, at the wrong time from your point of view.

♦ **What taxes are paid inside the investment product and what taxes will I be liable for on withdrawal?** Remember, creating wealth is about keeping money, not making money and you will need to take tax into account as you judge the real potential returns. Also, you personally may be exempt from a tax (for example, the DIRT exemption, which is means-tested for over 65s) that is being paid inside the product. If this is the case, may I suggest that you would be foolish to expose yourself to a tax that you should not be paying.

♦ **Whether there is borrowing inside the product and on what basis is it arranged?** Borrowing within such products can be on either a recourse or non-recourse basis. What this means is that the lender, in the event of the investment not going to plan, may (recourse) or may not (non-recourse) be able to demand more money from you, over and above the amount you originally committed. You need to know in advance whether there is any potential for you to be asked for more money, if the investment does not perform to plan.

♦ **If the investment fund is new (and thus lacks any real history), what is the fund manager's experience in the market where this investment takes place and what**

successes have they had in the past (albeit in a different fund)? New funds are more difficult to judge and remembering that it is people who manage money, not institutions or brand names, leads you to seek information on the people responsible in the particular project you are considering. These people's experience, both in the investment class (property, equity, gilts or cash) and in the jurisdiction (particularly important, if you are dealing with an Irish manager investing in an overseas market) are vitally important. You cannot be expected to invest your money with people who have no track record and/or no experience in the market being targeted.

As I write this, I feel I could go on and on thinking up questions for you to ask and I am sure you may well think of more than I have listed here. However, I believe I have covered all of the main areas and, if you have all these questions answered, the next time you are considering an off-the-shelf or manufactured investment project, you will make a more informed and better decision. Also, never forget that you want the answers in writing on the letterhead of the person or institution selling you the product.

3

Invest Tax-free

One of the simplest, and yet most effective, lessons I have learned over my years in the financial business is that creating wealth is about **keeping** money, not **earning** money – quite a different discipline. Most of the clients I meet in my working life are quite good at earning money, but are nowhere near as good at keeping it!

If you recognise the truth of this basic idea, then one of the wealth creation activities you must master is reducing your liabilities (the things that stop you from keeping more of the money you earn). While the liabilities in life are numerous and varied, and include our home (which consumes our income), our cars, our holidays, even our children, from a wealth-creation viewpoint, there is no doubt as to the greatest liability of all: tax.

Tax undermines our efforts to create wealth at nearly every turn. When we earn our money, we pay income tax; when we invest our money, we pay stamp duty; when we grow our investments, we pay capital gains tax. Not only this, but when we spend our money, we pay VAT and/or excise duties; and, even when we leave our money (or gift it) to our heirs, they pay capital acquisitions tax. Tax is the greatest liability in all of our lives and thus is the greatest obstacle to the accumulation of wealth. Therefore, although it may sound simplistic, the less tax we pay, the more opportunity we have for genuine wealth creation.

As I was first drafting this section (October 2006), the Irish Revenue had embarked on an advertising campaign to make people aware of their unclaimed tax concessions. Irish radio and TV ads claim that almost €1 billion in tax breaks remain unclaimed by the Irish tax payers. Revenue hotlines have been established to assist tax-payers who do not know how to claim their rightful rebates. This Revenue activity clearly demonstrates one of the points I want to raise around tax: you have a right to pay as little tax as legitimately possible.

I say this because, quite frankly, those people (generally referred to in newspaper articles by the collective noun, "the rich") who plan taxation and exercise their "right to pay as little as legitimately possible" have been attacked and vilified in the media. Indeed, there has been so much bad press around this subject that I believe many people, who could pay a lot less tax, have started to believe that to do so would be unpatriotic and detrimental to their fellow-citizens.

If you share this belief, then let me assure you that nothing could be further from the truth. The vast bulk of the media attention on this subject has been promoted by opposition parties in the Dáil. To understand why any feelings on your own part of being "unpatriotic" or "greedy" are misplaced, you must first understand the motivation of the promoters of such media coverage. There is only one reason why politicians sponsor such media hype – to win votes! Recognising the agenda of those promoting the negative stories allows one to ask whether they are telling the whole truth. When the "whole truth" delivers the politicians' vote-winning agenda, then they have no problem with it, but it should not surprise any reader that, when it does not suit their agenda, politicians can be very economical with the truth.

Let me explain, using a relatively recent headline I saw in one of the national newspapers. It read:

"Irish Landlords avoid €458m in Tax"

If memory serves, the article beneath the headline went on to claim this to be another "rich-get-richer-while-the-working-man-gets-poorer" story and the Labour Finance spokesman was quoted heavily. This article was not, in my opinion, an attempt to inform the reader, as it only told part of the story. Yes, the figures were accurate but only one of the relevant figures (relevant to the whole truth, that is, not to the sponsor's vote-winning agenda) was quoted, with the rest of the article dedicated to demonstrating how "unfair" this was and to suggesting that a Labour Government would *fix the problem*. Let me attempt to give you the other figures that are relevant to this story:

- To get the tax breaks, the landlords had to invest *circa* €1 billion into the Irish economy, mostly into property.

- When investing their €1 billion in Irish property, the landlords created income for the Irish Exchequer in the region of €135 million in VAT receipts.

- They further created *circa* €50 million in stamp duty for the Exchequer.

- They paid huge planning levies to local authorities, in return for planning permission.

- Thousands of jobs – for bricklayers, carpenters, architects and quantity surveyors, to name just a few – were created by the landlords' investment, with large amounts of income tax paid by those people on their salaries and income.

- Landlords and workers alike spent most of their net income in the Irish economy, paying huge amounts of VAT and excise duties as they did so.

As you can see, while the headline figure of €458 million was correct, the article "forgot" to mention the benefits enjoyed by the State and, for one, I am sure that those benefits far outweighed the costs. Of course, mentioning these spin-off benefits would neither make the story more interesting (and thus could not be seen as something that would sell more newspapers) nor would lend itself to the vote-winning agenda of the politician concerned.

I suggest that the benefits would not come as a surprise either to the journalist who wrote the article, nor to the politician who sponsored the piece, but they may come as a surprise to you? The bad press that tax breaks have been receiving can only be interpreted accurately when you know the motivation of the writer and/or the political contributor. Hopefully, you can see that, in reality, tax breaks benefit State and tax-payer alike. Thus, avoiding them out of some mis-guided patriotism, or out of a desire to not appear "greedy", is a false economy to us all. Think of it this way, without tax breaks, there would be very little tourist accommodation on our western seaboard and tourism in Ireland would be far less lucrative than it is. Without tax breaks, many of our elderly and infirm would not have a safe place to grow old with dignity. Without tax breaks, many working parents would have no place to leave their children during the day. I could go on and on but there is no need to labour the point any further. Tax breaks benefit people directly and, more importantly, indirectly. Many of those being targeted by the anti-tax break propaganda, despite not benefiting directly, benefit largely indirectly and, in my opinion, are having "the wool pulled over their eyes" by people with a very different agenda. The same people, by the way, were enraged by the reduction of Ireland's capital gains tax rate from 40% to 20%, once again promoting the idea that such a move only benefited "the rich". However, they stayed quiet when the reduction meant that the Exchequer received *circa* 10 times more tax after the rate reduction. The high level of tax had been a barrier to commercial activity and if "the rich" had not paid "10 times more", then the rest of us would have to have paid more ourselves.

So, it is neither unpatriotic nor detrimental to your fellow citizens for you to exercise your right to pay as little tax as legitimately possible!

RETIREMENT PLANNING

So, let us look at some ideas that will allow you pay less tax and create more wealth. The first port of call is retirement planning legislation. I believe that retirement allowances are not only the easiest tax breaks to access but, in many ways, they are the safest too. While such allowances do not apply to all income ("unearned" income, such as rental income from property or dividend income from shares, is not "pensionable"), they do apply to all "earned" income, whether you earn it as an employee in the PAYE system (which includes owner/managers of private limited companies) or as a sole trader.

Dealing with sole traders first, your retirement allowances are provided under Part 30 of the Taxes Consolidation Act, 1987, Section 787, which provides that, depending upon your age, you are permitted to invest a percentage of your income before tax and levies are applied. You must invest in an approved retirement plan, officially known as a retirement annuity contract (RAC), and the percentages are applied to your net relevant income. The allowable percentages are as follows:

Age Band	Annual Allowance
Under 30	15% of earnings
Age 30-39	20% of earnings
Age 40-49	25% of earnings
Age 50-54	30%* of earnings
Age 55-59	35%* of earnings
Above 60	40%* of earnings

Note: These allowances apply both to men and to women.

* Maximum earnings allowance in 2008 is €275,239, thus the maximum payment allowed by a sole trader is €110,095.60 (40% of €275,239).

So, for example, a 42-year-old with net relevant earnings of €100,000 *p.a.* could choose to invest €25,000 *p.a.* into an approved retirement structure. If he/she does this, due to the fact that this money is paid before tax and levies, the cost is considerably less than €25,000. Based on the top tax rate of 41% and levies of 5%, the out-of-pocket cost to this tax payer will be:

	€
Gross annual cost	25,000
Less tax & levies saved	(11,500)
Out-of-pocket cost	**13,500**

To put it another way, for a cost of €13,500, our wealth creator has an investment valued at €25,000 – an increase in wealth of 85% in a single day! In addition, all future income created within the retirement fund will be exempt from income tax and any future capital gains will be exempt from capital gains tax. So, when compared to paying the tax and investing the net €13,500 in your own name (which many people are doing right now – maybe you are one of them?), the retirement structure allows you to keep more of the money you earn and to keep more of the returns you receive on your investment. Compared to investing personally with far less money, where tax would be payable on all investment returns too, you will get wealthier using the retirement route.

For those readers who are employees, your retirement allowances also are provided under the Taxes Consolidation Act, 1987, although this time under Section 774, and the same personal allowances apply as for sole traders and thus the previous example would apply to you too. However, the advantage you have over the sole traders is that, in addition to your personal allowance, your employer will have a further allowance to pay on your behalf.

So, once again, assuming you are 42 years of age, you could invest up to 25% of your income before you pay tax and, in addition, your employer could invest another 100%+ (of your salary) on top. I am not for a moment suggesting that your employer is suddenly going to get considerably more generous, but this is something to bear in mind as you negotiate future salary increases. If, for example, you are lucky and/or good enough to negotiate a €10,000 increase in salary, assuming the top rate of tax and levies, you will keep no more than €5,400 of the increase. If, however, you decide to have the €10,000 put into a retirement plan on your behalf, you keep €10,000 (an 85% increase in wealth in a day) and that money is invested to create more wealth in the future. There is also an opportunity for you, once again by haggling, even to get a bit more, since it is cheaper for your employer to pay a retirement contribution than additional salary, as the employer does not pay employer's PRSI on the retirement contribution. Thus, if you choose to have future remuneration increases paid in the manner I suggest, in this example your employer will save €1,075 in PRSI. Perhaps you both can share this saving? If so, you might receive €10,537.50 into your retirement plan, a wealth increase of 98.82% when compared to taking the salary and paying the tax.

Those readers who are proprietary directors of their own limited company can take the greatest advantage of all. Again, taking an example of a 42-year-old and an overall allowance of *circa* 125% of declared salary (allowances for employees and owner/directors alike are individually approved by the Financial Services (Pensions) Business Unit of the Revenue Commissioners and may vary, depending upon age, sex and previously funded retirement benefits (hence the use of approximate figures here)). Therefore, if you declare a salary of, say, €50,000 *p.a.*, up to €62,500 *p.a.* could be invested into a retirement plan on your behalf. In effect, you receive an annual remuneration of €112,500 *p.a.*, but pay tax on only €50,000 of this figure. Even if we assume you pay the maximum tax and levy charge on the €50,000 (and, of course, you will not, as you have an annual tax credit and tax will be paid at 20% on some of this income), you pay income tax and levies of €23,000, an effective tax rate of just 20% on your total remuneration (salary plus pension).

In my experience, many owner/directors have kept salary declarations artificially low, believing it to be the only tax avoidance mechanism available to them. However, now you can see that, always assuming the cash is available within your company, it may actually pay to have a higher salary, as the more salary you declare, the more tax free cash can be moved to your retirement plan. Moving this cash not only means you get the benefit without tax interference, but the payment itself is treated as a trading expense within the company and thus leaves before corporation tax is levied.

Using your retirement allowances effectively allows you to alter considerably the way you pay yourself. Obviously, you need a certain salary to go through the tax system to fund your lifestyle (light and heat, home, car and travel expenses, holidays, clothing, etc) but one could argue that, at least until you have used all retirement allowances, you do not need to declare any more salary than covers these costs. A restructuring of how you remunerate yourself may be along the lines of having a basic salary that covers your lifestyle costs and an annual bonus linked to the profits your company makes. This type of remuneration structure, which would have to be formally documented and signed off by your Board of Directors, would mean that, when profits in your business were low, the basic salary would allow you to "pay the minimum amount of tax legitimately possible". Obviously, when profits are low (which could be due to trading difficulties, but could just as easily be due to major reinvestment of profits), there will be no money for your retirement fund and a contribution would not be paid (you need to pay attention to Revenue rules here that insist, over the full term of the retirement fund, on a certain amount of contribution being deemed a "regular contribution"). Conversely, when profits are high, your income would be dragged higher, allowing more tax-free contributions to be made to your retirement fund.

I want now to demonstrate the wealth creation power of retirement funds. In this example, consider a residential property investment, where you are buying an apartment for €250,000 over 15 years. I am assuming that you borrow 75% of the purchase price over the 15-year period, at an interest rate of 4.5% and that you enjoy 5% *p.a.* capital appreciation. Thus, in 15 years' time, you will be able to sell the property for €520,000 (rounded up to the nearest €1,000). My final assumption is that you will receive a rental yield of 3% *p.a.*, based on the initial purchase price, with the property assumed to be let for only 10 months each year. So, what will be the costs and real rates of return, if you buy this personally, as opposed to buying it through a retirement fund?

Purchase personally	€
Cash up-front (25% of purchase cost of €250,000)	62,500.00
Required monthly payment to lender (@ 4.5% interest)	1,454.90
Average monthly rent received (€250,000 x 3% = €7,500 = €625pm; 10 months' letting = €6,250, divided by 12 to give average monthly rent)	520.83
Average tax & levies (46%) on rent	49.49
Retained monthly rent	471.34
Total out-of-pocket cost of property (cash up-front + monthly payment to lender x 15 years less retained rent x 15 years)	239,540.80
Sales price of property in 15 years' time (@ 5% *p.a.* capital appreciation)	520,000.00
Capital Gains Tax on sale proceeds	54,000.00
Net sale proceeds to investor	466,000.00
Less total out-of-pocket cost of property	239,540.80
Net return to investor	226,459.20
Internal rate of return to investor on net return	**6.51%**

Note that the interest payments to the lender (which, in this example, would be an average of €453.23 per month, out of the €1,454.90 being paid monthly) are fully tax-deductible. I have reflected this tax deduction when calculating the tax payable on the rent.

So, as you can see, the borrower's gross payments (€62,500 upfront and €1,454.90 per month for 180 months), which total €324,382 over 15 years, net down to €239,540.80 once tax deductions and the tenant's rent are taken into account.

Now, let's look at the same purchase, but this time inside a private retirement fund.

Purchase through Retirement Fund	€
Lump sum contribution to retirement fund	62,500.00
Tax saving on lump sum contribution (@ 46%)	28,750.00
Out-of-pocket cost of cash up-front	33,750.00
Required monthly payment to lender	1,454.90
Average monthly rent received	520.83
Average tax & levies (46%) on rent	0.00
Required monthly regular contribution to retirement fund	934.07
Tax relief on regular contribution (@ 46%)	429.67
Out-of-pocket cost of monthly regular contribution	504.40
Total out-of-pocket cost of property (net lump sum contribution + regular contribution x 15 years)	124,542.00
Value of retirement fund in 15 years' time (property within fund)	520,000.00
Withdrawal tax (46%) on dissolution of retirement fund	179,400.00
Net value of retirement fund in 15 years' time	340,600.00
Less total out-of-pocket cost of property	124,542.00
Net return to investor	340,600.00
Internal rate of return to investor	**9.49%**

By altering "how" you purchase the property, the out-of-pocket costs of the purchase reduce from €239,540.80 in the previous example to €124,542.00 – a cost reduction of 49.5%! This is achieved by massively reducing the tax "costs" (one of the vital areas on which to concentrate) of paying the deposit (a net cost of €33,750 here instead of €62,500) and by removing both income tax from the rent and capital gains tax from the eventual sale. This cost reduction effectively increases the return by 45.8% (from 6.51% *p.a.* to 9.49% *p.a.*).

As you can see, by purchasing this property in a different way, through a retirement fund, you increase your internal rate of return (your rate of wealth creation, in effect) by over 45%. The property is the same, the capital appreciation and rental yields are the same, only the structure is different.

To take advantage of these benefits, you must qualify for the tax savings illustrated (which will depend on your employment status and salary declaration) but, at the very least, everyone should investigate whether this type of planning is available to them. Those employed by others and taxed *via* the PAYE system could enjoy this structure via an additional voluntary contribution (AVC) scheme, which is generally available alongside your main pension (superannuation) plan. The self-employed can benefit through the use of a self-invested personal pension (SIPP), while owner/managers of limited companies can do so via a self-administered retirement trust (SART).

While these schemes have some (limited) prohibitions on the type of investment that can be made, for the most part, any investment you can make in your own name can be made within your retirement plan too. Thus, anyone, no matter what your employment status, can, and in my opinion should, take some advantage. You will need the help of a real financial adviser and you will need to pay a fee for his/her services.

One word of caution here: fees vary widely in the marketplace and you should not simply opt for the cheapest you can get. Like most things in life, the cheapest is rarely the best and, in my experience, the cheaper the private retirement plan (a collective name for all such retirement funds), the more restrictive the product. Such plans can have very different terms and conditions (within the broad, Revenue-imposed, rules) and it is here that you need to pay considerable attention. At the time of writing, for example, I am aware of one stockbroking firm that will give you a SART for free, but their version only allows investment in products sold by that stockbroking firm. In order to be persuaded to pay any fee for such a product, personally I would have to be convinced that the adviser can provide all of the following:

♦ Where necessary, the adviser firm must be directly or indirectly[5] approved by the Financial Services (Pensions) Business Unit of the Revenue Commissioners as a pensioneer trustee. For both employees and owner-managers of limited companies, such a trustee is mandatory and is a requirement for Revenue approval; however trustees are not needed for the sole trader version of a private pension fund.

♦ Tax and remuneration planning services, so that you can take the maximum advantage possible from the opportunities such plans make available. Be sure that the firm you choose to deal with has in-house tax expertise.

♦ The investments allowed within the scheme have to be as broad as the Revenue allow, as restrictions imposed by some sellers of such schemes are "self-serving" and provide no benefits to you, the investor.

♦ Many such schemes require an annual, and independent, audit to be performed. Make sure that the firm you choose includes this service in the fees outlined.

♦ Some investment opportunities that may present themselves will require legal expertise, particularly where foreign investments are being considered (and here tax expertise may also be required), and the adviser you choose should demonstrate their ability to guide you in these areas. Legal expertise will also be necessary, from time to time, for Irish investments (for example, for property conveyancing).

♦ As with any investment plan, it will need to be reviewed on a regular basis, if only to ensure that what you have

---

5   That is, the adviser must have an affiliation to another adviser who provides this service.

invested in already remains the best option for you. Ensure such a service is available and that it is priced in advance.

♦ Under Revenue rules, some private retirement plans must be actuarially reviewed every three years. Make sure that the adviser firm you choose has the capabilities to perform this task and that the costs are included in the fees quoted.

If the adviser firm you eventually choose cannot provide these services, then you will have to purchase them separately, which will increase the costs. I see little point in going through this whole planning exercise, if much of the tax-saving benefits you enjoy are eaten away by professional fees being paid to multiple service providers.

OTHER PERSONAL, TAX CONCESSIONS

It is well beyond the scope of this book (or any other readable volume, I suggest) to outline every single tax concession available in the marketplace. Instead, in this section, I want to give you some idea of the considerable benefits that can be enjoyed when you use the tax legislation effectively and, thus, to motivate you to seek a meeting with a real financial adviser. Some readers will be able to enjoy benefits that, quite frankly, will amaze you, whilst other benefits will be of a more modest nature. However, as long as the fees payable do not erode the benefits to be enjoyed, any benefit you can take is worth investigation.

May I suggest that, at the least, if you do not investigate whether you can benefit from such planning, any subsequent decision you make will be ill-informed. I mentioned at the very start of this book that only when you have the full facts (the costs, the benefits and the risks) can you make financial decisions to your best possible advantage.

TAX RELIEF AGAINST RENTAL INCOME

Let's look at the wealth creation opportunities that the various tax breaks available against Irish rental income (including Section 23, Section 48 and other capital allowance schemes) offer.

First, let's assume that you have an existing Irish rental property, which you have held for a long time and thus no debt is outstanding. It has a value of €500,000 at present and you receive an annual rent of €12,500 (a 3% yield, but assuming you only get 10 months' rental a year). For the sake of the tax calculation, I am making two further assumptions:

♦ You spend €1,000 a year on maintaining the property.

♦ Your normal tax credits are used up by earned income (either PAYE or sole trader) elsewhere.

On these assumptions, the net income you currently receive may be calculated as follows:

	€
Gross annual rental income	12,500
Less deductible maintenance costs	1,000
Taxable annual income	11,500
Tax & levies (@ 46%)	5,290
Net annual income	**6,210**

For your €500,000 investment (whether you paid €500,000 or not is of no importance; there is now €500,000 of your capital at risk in this investment), you are receiving a net rental yield of just 1.24% *p.a.*, plus any capital appreciation of course.

Assuming that these figures are constant and that, over the next 10 years, you receive 5% *p.a.* capital appreciation, your internal rate of return (IRR) over the decade will be 6.07% *p.a.* Selling the property at that stage would trigger capital gains tax

(CGT) and, for our example, assuming the maximum amount of CGT would bring down the net IRR to 5.26% *p.a.*

Next, assume that a Section 23 property has been made available to you at a cost of €200,000, with tax allowances/qualifying relief of €170,000 (85% of the purchase price), but you have no cash available. What would happen to your IRR if you were to borrow the full €200,000 and buy the Section 23 property? Such a loan should be available on a full interest-only basis (you are providing the lender with €700,000 worth of property for a loan of just €200,000, a loan-to-value (LTV) of only 28.6%) and thus, assuming an interest rate of, say, 4.5%, the cost should be €9,000 *p.a.*

However, assuming the same rental yield on the new Section 23 property as the original property, you should receive a rental income of €5,000 *p.a.* There will be no tax to pay on this rental income as the interest-only payments exceed that income. So, the out-of-pocket expense of this new loan is just €4,000 *p.a.* (€9,000 cost of debt less €5,000 annual rent).

Now let us examine what happens to your tax calculation on the existing property:

	€
Gross annual rental income	12,500
Less deductible maintenance costs	1,000
Taxable annual income	11,500
Annual Section 23 tax allowances (€170,000 divided by 10)	17,000
Tax & levies (@ 46%)	Nil
Net annual income	**11,500**

So, in simple terms, for a net cost of €4,000 (the after-rent cost of the new loan), you receive additional income of €5,290 *p.a.* Continuing the simplistic analysis for a moment, one could view this as an "investment" of €4,000 *p.a.* yielding a "return" of €5,290 *p.a.*, an annual IRR of 35.13%.

Returning to the more complex calculation, again assuming our earlier figures remain constant over the next few years, but only assuming a capital gain on the original property (Section 23 properties can be overpriced due to the tax break, so assume it sells after 10 years for the original purchase price), what will be your long-term IRR?

Before taking account of a maximum CGT liability on the sale price of the original property, your IRR rises to 7.03% *p.a.* (a 15.8% total rise compared to the previous calculation) and to 6.24% after CGT (an 18.6% total rise in the real yield) However, if you can find a Section 23 property that is not overpriced and actually grows in value over the 10 years, then the IRRs will grow too.

Assuming a 3% rise (still a lesser assumption then the original property, as I am confident you will pay some premium on the purchase price to get the tax breaks) in the value of the Section 23 property will mean a value in 10 years of €268,784, creating additional wealth of €68,784 before CGT or €55,028 afterwards. This result would increase your IRR on the overall project to 7.84% *p.a.* before CGT (an increase of 29.2% in the total real yield) and 6.94% *p.a.* (a 31.8% total rise in real yield) after all taxes.

Hopefully, you can see that, without necessarily taking on hugely increased risks, it is possible to alter substantially the wealth creation effect of existing investments. When I ran these numbers for the first time, it struck me that, in the original one-property, no-debt, situation, the rewards being "enjoyed" by the investor (a net rental yield of just 1.24% and a net overall IRR of 5.26% *p.a.*) were those one would expect from extremely low risk (deposit-style) investments. There is no way, may I suggest, that the investor is being rewarded for the investment risk, as the real returns could be achieved by simply placing the cash on long-term deposit. By changing "the way that you do it", you are simply putting yourself in the way of the increased rewards that you deserve for the risk being taken.

At the time of writing, there are a number of tax schemes (in addition to the purchase of a Section 23 property) that could deliver similar advantages – for example, certain capital allowance schemes (generally, making tax breaks available through investment in nursing homes, crèche facilities and hotels), the tax allowances of which generally are available against Irish rental income only.

Remember, too, that saving tax will only make you truly wealthier if you invest the savings. In our last example, simply saving €1,405 *p.a.* in tax will make a modest difference to your lifestyle if you spend it, but investing the savings and receiving a 5% *p.a.* growth will accumulate a further €18,555 at the end of the 10 year term, further increasing your true IRRs.

TAX–FREE ROLL–UP FUNDS

In **Chapter 1**, we discussed off-the-shelf investment products and you are now armed to make much better, and more informed, investment decisions.

When investing either lump sums or regular contributions (and assuming you have used the direct tax breaks available and/or suitable in your circumstances), putting taxation at the centre of your decision-making process will lead you back to the door of the off-the-shelf product manufacturers, because many such manufacturers have tax-free roll-up funds.

Under the broad banner of life insurance legislation, it is possible for you to invest money and, as long as the money stays within the chosen product (subject to the "8-year rule" outlined below), pay neither income tax on any income earned, nor capital gains tax on any gains made. Compare this to personally-held investments, where up to 46% of the income and 20% of the gains can be lost to taxation, and you can immediately see that there may be substantial benefits for you in using such funds.

While there is no income tax or capital gains tax to pay *within* these products, exit tax at the rate of 23% of "profit" is charged on *withdrawal*.

There have been recent changes to the tax treatment of these products, where every eight years (hence the "8-year rule"), if you hold the investment that long, the profits are deemed to have been paid out to you (whether they leave the investment or not) and taxed at the 23% rate.

To illustrate the potential benefits of these structures, let us look at investments in the stock market. Assume an investor wishes to place €100,000 into the stock markets and, although he/she wants the ability to buy and sell stocks as necessary, overall they have a 15-year investment term in mind. Assume their investment receives a pre-tax return of 7% *p.a.* and further assume half of this annual growth will be income, the other half capital gain – tax is calculated at an overall rate of 33% on the annual yield. On this basis, the investor's accumulated wealth in 15 years' time will be approximately €197,880.

Tax has had the effect of reducing the accumulated future value by €78,024, which, when expressed as a percentage of the gain the investor keeps, is a reduction of 79.7%. The fact that tax is paid year by year (and thus the investor has less money invested over the full term) means that, even when we assume a tax rate of 33%, the investor's ultimate profit reduces by more than double the tax rate.

Choosing to make the investment within a tax-free roll-up fund means that, as tax is only payable twice (once at the end of year 8 and again seven years later), more money is invested for longer. Tax will be payable at an exit rate of only 23% (half the marginal rate of income tax plus levies and only 3% higher than CGT). Thus, using the same growth assumption of 7% *p.a.*, the investor's tax-paid fund in 15 years will be worth €227,740.

Comparison tells us that the investor keeps €29,860 more, or put another way, €1,990.67 *p.a.* more. As long as the costs of the off-the-shelf product are less than this amount, and your new-found knowledge will allow you to judge the real costs, then the way you make the investment will alter the result you achieve.

Such products offer a wide range of underlying investments, from individual and/or groups of direct stock market holdings, to pooled investment funds covering property, cash deposits (although the tax benefits may not be so lucrative due to the deposit interest retention tax (DIRT) rate being only 20%) and corporate or national loan paper (gilts).

FORMALLY RECOGNISING FAMILY MEMBERS' INPUT

Until relatively recently, in Ireland, most married tax-payers were actively encouraged to declare just one income, as such a declaration would mean less effort in preparing tax returns. In addition, there was little or no financial benefit to declaring two separate incomes, but all of that changed in the Finance Act 2001. The then Minister for Finance, Charlie McCreevey, introduced the individualisation of tax credits and, immediately, there was a benefit to declaring two separate incomes.

To illustrate the benefit, let me use the example of Joe, a married man earning €100,000 *p.a.* in PAYE income from his own limited company (this example could apply just as well to a sole trader). At present, assuming Joe receives the basic tax credits and home loan mortgage interest relief, he will take home €75,015. Joe's wife actively works in the business but they have always declared only one income. However, his twin brother, Mike, is setting up a new business and has received advice that he and his wife each should have an income, up-to-the-minute advice that his brother has not yet received. Thus, having learned of the benefits of individualisation, Mike's wife will have a salary of €20,000, while Mike will earn €80,000. Although both households earn the same amount of money (€100,000), once again, using standard tax credit and relief assumptions, Mike and his wife will take home €81,045 (Mike will take home €63,215 of his salary, while his wife will take home €17,830). So, by paying attention to the way income is declared, Mike and his wife get to keep 8% more and have €5,030 *p.a.* to invest towards wealth creation that Joe and his wife do not have.

Of course, for the family with just one income to enjoy the benefits of such planning is not necessarily as simple as reducing one salary and paying the other spouse that amount as a second salary. Simply reducing your salary without some acceptable reason may not impress the Revenue Commissioners (who might perceive the move as aggressive tax avoidance) but, if such an action is taken as part of a complete restructuring of remuneration and is done in a formal manner with supporting employment contracts and Board resolutions, then the benefits can be enjoyed.

Not only is there the immediate benefit, but there could be considerable knock-on benefits too. For the limited company owners, where a maximum fund cap of €5,418,085 (to be indexed each year) is placed on private retirement funds, the retirement planning cap effectively is increased to €10.8 million, as there are now two people for whom private retirement funds can be provided. A sole trader, whose annual contributions to private retirement funds are dictated by legislation (see page **42**) and limited to a percentage of €275,239 *p.a.* in taxable income, by formally recognising a spouse's contribution to the business, can more than double their retirement fund allowances.

To take advantage of these benefits, you do not need to work for yourself. Personal tax credits (different from "allowances") are also available against rental income. Although I often find that rental properties are held in the name of the income-earning spouse (generally, the husband), transferring the property (and thus the income) to the spouse will allow his/her individual tax credits to be applied against the rental income, with the same resulting benefit. So, for the employed person who is attempting to build wealth outside their principal place of employment, holding assets in a spouse's name may be the best course of action, at least to the extent that the income created is adequate to use the maximum tax credits.

Furthermore, benefits could also accrue, especially to business owners, by employing your adult children. Many readers will have children over the age of 18, who are costing a fortune in after-tax income. College fees and living expenses have to be paid and most people in this situation make these payments out of after-tax income. Why not give these children a job – as long as there is some job that they can do? Under current tax rules, they may earn up to €18,300 *p.a.* and pay no tax whatsoever (if you give them this money out of your own pocket, you have to earn approximately €33,890, assuming 46% tax and levies), thus paying them a salary could save €15,590 *p.a.*

The reason, in my view, that most people pay more tax than they need to is that neither they nor their existing advisers are aware of the legitimate ways of reducing their burden. Furthermore, neither they nor their existing advisers are willing to invest the time in improving their knowledge or the time required to act on these new ideas. Such actions, generally speaking, are mundane and definitely less exciting than activities that either create or spend income. Paperwork is required, registrations with the Revenue and other State authorities are needed, financial advisers need to be sought out and interviewed, assets have to be moved from one name to another; in short, it all seems like too much hassle. Indeed, let's call a spade a spade: the truth is that it is hassle and unexciting but, if you keep your eye on the benefits, it is certainly not "too much hassle".

If you are happy with the amount of tax you pay, then, of course, you need change nothing. However, if you are not happy, then recognise this one simple truth:

"Tomorrow, you are going to have to do something different than you did yesterday."

While, I hope, this chapter has shown you many ways of keeping more money, it is not always necessary or prudent to do-it-yourself. If you have neither the time nor the inclination, then pay someone else to do it for you. As long as the fee paid is less than the benefit you receive, then in essence, you are making money for free! If, for example, for every €10 you save in tax, the cost to you is €5, so what? You are still €5 better off and you'll get much wealthier much quicker if you can "buy tenners for fivers".

4
TURN YOUR BUSINESS INTO AN INVESTMENT ASSET

I believe it was Napoleon who coined the phrase "a nation of shop-keepers" when describing Britain, and there is no doubt that Ireland could be just as accurately described since a very large percentage of the Irish population is "self-employed" However, in my experience, very few of these people treat their business as an investment.

I will use a conversation I had recently with a motor dealer, which went something like this:

Me: *"How much is your business worth?"*

Motor dealer (proudly): *"€8m."*

Me: *"And what kind of a yield do you get from your €8m investment?"*

Motor dealer (confused): *"What do you mean?"*

Me: *"Does it provide you with any income?"*

Motor dealer (slightly defensive): *"Yes, of course. I pay myself €80,000 per year."*

Me: *"How many hours a week do you work?"*

Motor dealer (again proudly): *"50 to 60, I suppose."*

Me: *"So, let's forget it is a business for a moment and pretend it is an investment opportunity I am bringing to you for consideration."*

Motor dealer (with growing interest): *"OK. I'll play along."*

Me: *"I have an investment opportunity for you here, the broad details of which are: you'll invest €8m of your money with 100% risk to your capital – in other words, you could lose it all; I'll give you a 1% p.a. yield on your investment before tax, which will be about 0.5% p.a. after tax. However, to get the yield, you'll need to come to work for me for a minimum of 50 hours a week. What would you tell me to do with the investment?"*

Motor dealer (with realisation): *"I'd tell you where to shove it!"*

Me: *"And you'd be right, but isn't that what you are doing every day in your business?"*

While I cannot tell you exactly what the motor dealer said, you can use your imagination! Indeed, if you are a business owner, you may well be running your own numbers in your head, but please do not be too hard on yourself. You are, after all, in the majority. Ireland is filled with wealthy businesses and relatively poor owners of those businesses. In our example, the truth of the matter is that our motor dealer could sell his business, pay 20% CGT on the proceeds and be left with a cash sum of *circa* €6.4m (I have assumed the full sale price would be subject to tax). He could then place the cash on long-term deposit and get, after DIRT, at today's rates, an annual income of *circa* €192,000 (nearly five times his current net income) and never have to work again. So, with massively reduced risk, he could have massively increased income and a much improved lifestyle.

I am not for a moment suggesting that everyone in such a position should sell up to live the life of Reilly although, for some, that is a legitimate option to be considered. Doing so would ignore the potential capital appreciation that, in our example, the €8m may produce as the motor dealer grows his business further. Doing so may also ignore the long-term wishes of the business owner, who has an ambition to pass on his/her business to sons and daughters. However, as I had to do myself with my business, *Financial Engineering Network Ltd.*, I am suggesting that you recognise the following issues:

♦ If your business is completely dependent upon you, then it is unlikely to have any real sale value unless you are willing to sell yourself along with it.

♦ If you wish to leave it, or pass it on in your lifetime, to your family, unless you increase your yields, you will always have to draw an income and may become an unproductive financial drain on the business just when it is being passed to younger, less experienced, owners.

These are certainly two of the problems I faced when considering my own financial freedom. To copper-fasten the notional value of my business (the €8m in the motor dealer example), I needed to do two things:

♦ Over a period of time, to reduce my business's dependency upon me.

and/or

♦ To increase substantially the real yield I was getting from my business so that I could create separate, personal, wealth from which I could draw income in the future.

I choose to do both, as doing so meant I would be able to choose either to sell (without having to sell myself with the business) or to maintain my equity (a separate stream of income could be created without a sale).

REDUCING YOUR BUSINESS'S DEPENDENCY ON YOU

I remember having a conversation with one of Ireland's best known management consultants many years ago and asking him: *"Why is it that most small businesses never become larger businesses?"*

He thought about it for a moment, and then surprised me with a one-word answer: *"Ego"*.

He then expanded on his answer, telling me that many entrepreneurs are top-class ideas people, top-class risk-takers, top-class salespeople, top-class problem-solvers: *"But not necessarily top-class business or people managers. However, such people believe in their own abilities so much that they develop the opinion that they can do anything better than the next guy"*.

What he was saying was that they thought nobody could run their business better than they could and this very attitude meant it never dawned on them that perhaps someone could.

I immediately saw the sense in what he was saying, although, like most entrepreneurs, at the same time, I felt that gnawing feeling in the pit of my stomach. If left to its own devices, that gnawing feeling would have had me tell him he didn't know what he was talking about and, of course, nobody could run my business as well as I could. But, luckily for me, I kept that feeling under control and listened with my head and not my heart. Immediately, I decided to have a meeting with my fellow shareholders to discuss the idea.

We met at Christmas-time, 2002. In a Dublin hotel, and over the customary few pints, I told them of my recent encounter with the management consultant. They too felt the gnawing feeling in their stomachs but they too put their emotions aside and listened to the *real* question, which was: *"What do we want our business to be? A good one that provides us with a reasonable standard of living (as it was already doing in 2002), but of little real value in and of itself? Or, a much larger business that could stand on its own two feet and, eventually, could provide us all with the real financial freedom we so greatly desired?"*

To use a phrase that one of my business partners is quite fond of, especially when he is taking minutes of a formal meeting, "an elongated and heated discussion ensued", at the end of which we all agreed, we wanted the bigger business that would have real embedded value (separate from its shareholders/directors).

Having made this decision, we quickly came to the conclusion that none of us were trained in running a business; we were, after all, simply financial advisers. To turn our business into a large, professionally-managed, properly-structured entity that could deliver the intellectual property of the founders through a network of Dublin and regionally-based advisers, would take a skill-set that we simply did not possess. Either, we agreed, one of us would have to invest a number of years in educating himself to the required level of expertise or we would have to hire the expertise from outside.

Whether it was laziness or an unwillingness to wait on our part, I cannot remember, but we decided on the latter. New expertise would be recruited into the business. We also recognised very quickly that, if this person was to have every incentive to succeed in his/her efforts, his/her goals would have to be aligned with our own. What was good for us would have to be good for him/her and *vice-versa*; otherwise, we would end up working on different agendas and in different directions (remember the non-alignment of goal issue discussed earlier between financial product-sellers and their customers).

I have an uncle who is involved in the pub and nightclub business and he told me something, when I was just 16 years old and working in his hotel as a lounge-boy, that has stuck with me ever since. He said that a good bar manager would work for you for five years maximum as, over that time, if he was really good, he would accumulate enough money to open his own bar. He was not only referring to the legitimate ways such an individual could accumulate money (such as tips and salary) but that he would find ways of "feathering his own nest". Deals with the drinks providers (this was the 1970s, after all) could line the bar manager's pockets, "sweetheart" arrangements with friends and family for special events and functions provided other opportunities, etc. I remember thinking at the time, but being too afraid to say anything to my hugely successful and very well-off uncle, that, if he shared some profit with his bar manager, he would gain two benefits:

♦ The good bar manager would stay well beyond five years and his bar would run consistently well and gain a reputation for doing so.

♦ The "sweetheart" deals would form part of my Uncle's profit, so increasing his return.

I did not think of this as an "alignment of goals" back in 1978, but that is what I meant.

In deciding to treat our business as an investment, we had to recognise that an "alignment of goals" was of paramount importance in achieving those goals. We would have to part with some shareholding to this new person so that, as their activities made us wealthier, he/she became wealthier too. Luckily, we knew that the ceding of equity did not necessarily require the simultaneous ceding of control (as shares can easily be split into "value" and "voting" shares – see the section on *Share Capping* in **Chapter 8**) and thus, from a control point of view, there would be no change. Also, we had to get the egos out of the way and remind ourselves that, as long as the underlying value of the shares we retained was greater than the original value (of 100% of the original shares), then we would be getting richer. The percentages no longer mattered, everything was now about the value.

By August 2003, we had recruited a new managing director (he replaced me in that role, another decision that meant the ego being left aside), a youthful gentleman, like ourselves, who had the skills required and a track record of taking smaller financial services businesses and turning them into larger, more valuable, entities. To get the right person, we had to build an attractive package and, while of course I cannot tell you the detail, I can give you a broad outline of how it worked:

◆ He would be paid a basic salary that was considerably less than the one he currently enjoyed. Indeed, it worked quite simply: we asked how much he needed to run his lifestyle and we paid a gross salary that would net down to that basic requirement.

◆ He, together with the original shareholders, wrote a three-year business plan for our business, the achievement of which would substantially increase the underlying value of our business.

◆ We agreed that every year for those three years, always assuming he was delivering on the business plan, he would be granted a certain percentage of the value shares in our business. Of course, we knew that, if he achieved his benchmarks, although we were giving away shares, those retained by us would be substantially more valuable.

◆ We agreed that, assuming all benchmarks were achieved, in three years' time, his remuneration package would be reviewed once more and a new plan would be worked out.

Of course, many reading this will think we were over-generous and that such a lucrative package would not be necessary just to hire a managing director. However, neither I nor my partners were looking for an ordinary managing director – we were looking for an **extraordinary** one. He had to have a proven track record, the required educational background and he had to be willing to take on a fair degree of risk. We wanted to be sure that whoever promised us that he/she could do what we asked, would be willing to "put his money where his mouth is" and to join us in the risk being taken. We found that person, we did our deal and, without revealing too much, I can tell you that the value of my shares in our business has more than doubled in the last four years (notwithstanding that, today, my percentage stake is a fair bit less than it was in August 2003).

In addition to the benefit of growing the value of the business, the very act of hiring the new managing director has diminished our company's dependency on its original shareholders. We are well on the way to a point in time where the business could be sold without us having to sell ourselves with it.

I do not present my own experience as something that all privately-owned businesses should replicate, but simply as an outline of what can be done to separate your business value from your own work effort. As said before, if you cannot do this, then the value you place on your business is merely notional, as it cannot be unlocked without you committing yourself to working for much longer than necessary.

Many readers will not want to sell their business ever, whether a sale is possible or not. If this applies to you, then replicating what we have done in *Financial Engineering Network Ltd.* would achieve little. Some businesses never attain a real value at all (whether a top-class manager is present or not), while others are ear-marked to pass on to the next generation. If you are one of these business-owners the only way to secure your own financial future is to increase the "yield" you get from that business and to invest the additional yield. In this way, over time, you will use your business to create a separate wealth pool that, in the future, will provide you with the income you need. If you can achieve this, when you come to stop working, you can either shut the door of your business and go home or pass on the business to your children without having to draw an income from it for the rest of your life.

The main reason (other than having no money, of course), in my experience, that owner-directors do not draw larger amounts from their business is income tax. About the only tax avoidance mechanism they have used in the past is not to declare income. However, you have already seen in **Chapter 3** that taking more money from your business does not necessarily lead to the payment of more income tax.

Here is where your private pension fund comes to the fore. May I suggest that it is time for you to seek out a *real* financial adviser and to pay him/her to show you how to use retirement planning legislation to build a separate wealth pool. The workings of these private retirement funds are well-explained in an earlier chapter so I do not intend to go into them again here. But, as you choose the adviser to assist you, ensure he/she has the ability to offer advice and service across all of the areas mentioned earlier.

Other tax concessions can be dovetailed with the use of your retirement allowances to increase the amounts that can be accumulated in a tax-free environment. In **Chapter 3**, for example, I mentioned Capital Allowance schemes, some of which, where earned income is concerned, could allow an additional annual tax credit of €31,750 for six years and €21,167 in the seventh (and final) year. If the cash is available in your company, and assuming your retirement allowance is 100% of your declared salary, arguably you could increase your income by €211,667 over the next seven years. Because you bought the tax break in advance, there would be no tax to pay and a further €211,667 could be moved to your retirement fund over the same period. In effect, you have increased your remuneration by €423,334 over the seven-year term and not paid a single penny in additional income tax. I do not offer this as a recommendation for all owner/manager-readers, since your own particular circumstances will dictate what you could and should do, but offer it merely as an example of what planning taxation could do for the real yields you are getting from your business.

RETAINING PROFIT WITHIN YOUR BUSINESS

Sections 598 and 599 of the Taxes Consolidation Act, 1987 outline a tax concession for business owners, designed to allow them to retire without having to pay an unreasonable amount of tax. Known as retirement relief, it allows an owner (either a sole trader or of a limited company) to receive up to €750,000 tax-free as they divest themselves of their business assets. To qualify for this concession, you must meet all the qualifying criteria, the most important of which are:

- You have reached the age of 55 or over.
- You have worked in the business for a period of five years or more.
- You have held effective ownership of the business (or a percentage of the business) for 10 years or more.

Note that this relief is only available if the full amount received is €750,000 or less. Although qualifying individuals who get a little more than the €750,000 can benefit from retirement relief, I do not want to give the impression to any reader that they automatically will receive €750,000 of any gain tax-free. If you sell your business for, say, €5 million, you will pay tax on the lot – retirement relief only applies to business owners who are selling for relatively small amounts.

The fact that this is a personal tax concession leads me to my first suggestion: if you are married, your spouse should own a percentage of the business (offering the opportunity of €1.5m in tax relief instead of just €750,000) and, especially if he/she is not employed elsewhere, he/she should be employed in the business too. Earlier, you saw that the legitimate employment of a non-earning spouse allows you to keep more income, now it may also afford you the opportunity to keep more capital too!

So you can see, especially over the last few years of your own working life, that it may well pay you to retain profits within the company so that, as you "retire", you can draw them out (either through liquidation or onward sale) tax-free. However, accumulating profits within a business can expose those profits (and the further income they may produce as they are invested within the company) to surcharges and/or additional Corporation Tax, all of which are costs to be taken into account as you investigate whether this type of planning would benefit you. Pure mathematics will be your guide here; you need to run the numbers (or pay someone else to do it for you) and decide whether you are better off to take the distributable profit on an ongoing basis or whether you will pay less tax (keep more money) if you retain those profits over a period of time and take advantage of retirement relief at the end.

5
STRUCTURE YOUR BUSINESS TO ACCUMULATE WEALTH

One of the few criticisms I received of my last book (*The Tricks of the Rich*) was from a number of accountants over what I said about sole tradership. In that book, as I am about to do in this one, I came down firmly on the side of limited companies, stating that: *"I can think of no reason why anyone, other than some business activities that cannot incorporate under Irish law, would operate as a sole trader."*

The accountants reminded me of the following facts, as they saw them:

- A sole tradership is less expensive to establish and run than a limited company.

- A sole tradership is less complex than a limited company, especially where corporate law and compliance are concerned

- A limited company can be established later, once surplus profits are being made.

I cannot disagree with these simple "facts" but, in *The Tricks of the Rich*, I was not writing about reducing costs! Neither was I (nor am I now) writing about reducing complexity. I was writing (and continue to write) about accumulating wealth and, in that context, I stand over my statement.

Any financial decision, in my view, must be made with all costs, benefits and risks taken into account and the near automatic advice to start your business life as a sole trader seems to concentrate solely on costs.

As I see them, the benefits of a limited company and the risk reduction effects of such a structure can be summarised as follows:

BENEFITS	RISK REDUCTION
Corporation tax is lower than personal income tax and thus, when it comes to building a better and more valuable business, a limited company can keep and reinvest more of its profit.	The financial risk taken by the business owner is limited to the cash (shareholders' funds) he/she invests in the business. There is no limit to the financial risk taken by a sole trader.
Corporation tax is payable six months after the business year-end, while sole traders pay the bulk of taxes two months before their year end. Thus, there is much more time to plan taxation within a limited company.	In the event of any legal action against your business in the future, such action is more likely to be aimed at the limited company itself than at the owner(s) of the company.
The various, legitimate, methods of tax reduction are far more wide-ranging and lucrative to the business owner within a limited company structure.	Other than in fraudulent trading cases, the concept of 'limited liability' remains intact in a limited company, no matter what financial results your business produces.
The ability to separate oneself from one's business can provide other planning opportunities along the route to wealth accumulation; one such area could be around VAT registration.	Once your limited company achieves a certain turnover level, the 'risk' of tax compliance is shared, at least in part, by the auditor of the business.

From a wealth accumulation perspective, there is no doubt in my mind that a limited company structure allows the owners of the business to keep more money and to reduce risk at the same time.

To suggest that this can be done "later, once surplus profits are being made" is akin, in my mind, to suggesting to a horse-owner that "you can always bolt the stable door after the horse has made its escape". If, at the start of any business venture, you cannot see yourself making profit, then perhaps you should not be moving forward with the idea at all rather than doing so as a sole trader, so that, if it does fail, you will lose less.

At the very least, I suggest that any business-owner, whether starting now or simply reviewing the current sole trader structure, should compare these benefits and reduction in risks against the costs. The Financial Regulator has one main *mantra* on financial advice, which is: *"If it is not in writing, it does not exist"*.

In reviewing, or deciding on, business structures, therefore, may I suggest that you ensure that any adviser puts his/her advice in writing and that the written advice includes an analysis of all costs, all benefits and all risks. If it is not in writing and does not analyse all relevant issues, as far as I am concerned, it is neither all-encompassing advice nor, according to the Regulator, "advice" at all.

For those who are forced down the sole trader route, either by legislation and/or by professional associations, bear in mind that such compulsion may not apply to every business activity in which you engage. For example, accountants must deliver audits as a sole trader (or partnership), but many such professionals are involved in other business activities that need not be delivered in the same manner. Other examples include the GP fraternity, where many general practices are turning into medical clinics and providing additional services to their patients through limited companies. The same could apply to dentists, orthodontists and solicitors, all of whom currently are compelled to offer their core services *via* the sole trader structure.

OTHER BUSINESS STRUCTURE IDEAS

In **Chapter 3**, the idea of formally recognising the efforts of your spouse and/or other family members in your business, whether sole trader or limited company, was discussed. For the sole traders amongst you, this opens the door to providing retirement plans for these "employees", retirement plans that will allow much more money to leave the business, tax-free, than could be invested in your own retirement plan.

Renting from "Oneself"

For professional practices, where the practitioner owns the building the practice occupies, the lack of the ability to pay oneself rent (which, if paid to a third party, would leave the practice tax-free) also hampers wealth accumulation. In such circumstances, consideration should be given to transferring the property to one's spouse (there is no stamp duty charged on property transfers between spouses) and creating a genuine lease between the new owner and the practice.

To illustrate the potential savings that this type of planning may produce, let us first look at the costs of repaying a loan, taken out by the practice proprietor, to fund the purchase of the practice premises. Assume a €500,000 loan to purchase the premises, taken out over 15 years at an interest rate of 5%. A standard loan structure, capital and interest style, applies. The cost of the loan will be:

	€
Monthly payment to lender	4,014.16
Average tax savings on interest within repayments (@ 46%)*	581.15
Net monthly cost	3,433.11
Cost to practice owner over 15 year term	**617,960.12**

* The interest element of this loan is fully allowable for tax purposes. This figure represents the tax the practice owner does not pay due to the loan being in place. Put another way, if the loan had not been taken out, the practice owner would have paid a total of €104,607 more tax (€581.15 x 180 months) over the 15 years.

So, the practice owner in this example has to earn a total of €617,960.12 (after tax, which, based on a total tax and levies cost of 46%, requires €1,144,370 in gross earnings) over the next 15 years.

Now, let us look at the same figures if the property is bought, not by the practice owner but by his/her spouse. The spouse becomes an employee of the practice and up to €18,300 of the money he/she needs to repay the loan can be paid as salary. This amount, based on all personal tax credits, can be earned by the spouse tax-free and, of course, leaves the practice before the owner pays tax. With his/her new-found knowledge, the practice owner, together with his/her spouse, has decided to repay the loan *via* a retirement-backed structure (interest-only

plus contributions to a retirement fund). The cost of the loan (on
the same assumptions as above) will be:

	€
Monthly payment to lender (interest-only)	2,083.33
Monthly regular contribution to retirement fund *	2,578.30
Total monthly cost	**4,661.63**

*   *As the spouse will pay tax on 75% of the retirement fund when it is accessed
in 15 years' time, this payment, based on an assumed 6% p.a. growth within
the fund, will accumulate €763,359 inside the fund, which will net down to
€500,000 after tax and levies (@ 46%) are paid (on 75%) on withdrawal.*

From the practice owner's point of view, all of this money can be
paid to his/her spouse out of pre-tax income. The make-up of the
payments is:

	€
Monthly salary to spouse	1,525.00
Monthly regular contribution to retirement fund for spouse	2,578.30
Monthly rent to spouse *	558.33
Monthly total payments	4,661.63
Average monthly tax savings **	2,144,35
Net monthly cost	2,517.28
Cost to practice owner over 15 year term	**453,100.44**

*   *This figure is calculated as the balance needed by the spouse, in addition to
salary, to meet the cost of interest payments to the lender. Because the loan is
on a rented property, the interest is fully allowable for tax and so no tax is
payable on this additional income.*

** *As salary, rent and retirement contributions for employees are all legitimate
trading expenses, all of these payments are made out of the practice owner's
gross income, thus increasing the tax effectiveness of this structure.*

Comparing this method to the normal one (the one the banks want you to use, as it creates more profit, with less risk for them, not for you), by paying attention to the way the loan is structured, and in this case to the person to whom it is granted, reduces the cost by €164,849.68 or, put another way, by 26.7%!

As with most examples I use in this book, I offer this one to demonstrate the potential benefits of paying attention to the *way* you do things, not to tell every reader to implement these changes in their current circumstances immediately. To make such changes legitimately, so that they are acceptable to the Revenue and lenders alike, will require specific advice and planning around your specific circumstances. However, this said, every married practice owner who personally owns his/her practice premises will be able to reap some benefits from such a planning exercise and with potential savings in high six-figure sums (based on a loan of €500,000, all other amounts being proportionate), surely it is worth your while investigating the benefits you might reap?

More importantly, I also give this example for people who have not yet made the error of placing property in the wrong names. While Revenue practice may make it impossible for some property owners to enjoy the benefits if they restructure existing property holdings (hence the suggestion that you need truly professional advice and assistance), the benefits outlined here are absolutely guaranteed if you plan your next property purchase with these benefits in mind. This should not stop existing property owners from seeking advice to see whether they can restructure, but I hope it will mean that, the next time you consider a property purchase of any kind, you pay as much attention to *how* you would hold such property as to *which* property you might buy.

Limited Companies for Property Owners

Many property owners that I come across in my professional life have decided to hold investment properties within a specially created limited company. Many other business owners have property sitting on the balance sheets of their trading companies.

The first question I put to such investors is *"Why?"*. Typically, the answer I receive is one (and in some cases, both) of the following:

◆ Taxation is far lower within a limited company and a sell-on later (of the company and not the property/ies)) will attract less stamp duty.

◆ At the time, I could not have afforded the property personally (recognising the issue I raised earlier of wealthy companies and relatively poor owners of said companies).

I usually address these answers in the following manner.

In the first case, I attempt to discover whether the decision was an isolated one around ongoing taxation and whether it was made purely with the basic tax rates in mind. Of course, it is true that holding property in one's personal name can mean taxation and levies, on exposed rental income, being charged at a rate of 46%. Comparing this to the maximum tax rate of 25% within an investment company on such income (the same rate applies even within trading companies that typically pay corporation tax at 12.5%), one would be forgiven for opting for the lower rate. However, have all costs been taken into account or has a relatively simplistic, isolated, decision actually allowed some inefficiencies creep into this property investor's world?

The other costs that should have been considered are:

◆ Although the limited company pays tax of at least the 25% rate on its exposed investment income, if the net income creates surplus profit in that company, which is paid out to the owners, they will pay further income tax and levies at up to 46%.

♦ If the limited company, to avoid the secondary tax liability, simply chooses not to distribute the investment profit, after 18 months a surcharge is levied on the undistributed income. In effect, the Revenue penalise the business owner for not drawing profits available for distribution that would give rise to charge to tax and levies at 46% on that distribution.

♦ While, in theory, the structure may lower stamp duty in the eventual sale, this will only happen if the owner can sell the shares in the company. In many cases I have seen (admittedly, in more recent times), buyers are refusing to purchase shares in private limited companies, preferring instead to purchase the assets of the business itself. The reason for this seems to be self-protection, in that the purchase of a company can expose the purchaser to a multitude of risks. For example, any outstanding legal action against the company could fall into the lap of a new owner, so too could any historical issues with employees, Revenue, creditors, etc. While all such potential liabilities could be dealt with via an indemnity to the buyer from the vendor, many buyers are unwilling to accept such indemnities as, from their perspective, such an indemnity can mean that their own financial future is somewhat dependent upon the financial ability of a third party. From the vendor's perspective, especially one who is selling due to retirement and who is seeking a financial future containing less risk, an open-ended indemnity maintains a degree of risk that may be neither welcome nor sensible. Thus maintaining property within a limited company, in the hope of some onward selling advantage at a future date, does not guarantee the advantage.

♦ The "sting in the tail", as it were, of holding property inside a limited company is the potential for double taxation as the property assets are sold on. Should any

future buyer insist on buying the assets and not the
company, the company must sell the property/ies and pay
its CGT liability of 20%. Then the owner must liquidate the
company and pay a further 20% CGT. This double tax
knock is one of the greatest potential costs of holding
property through a limited company.

By now, it will not surprise you to find out that, at times, we
make financial decisions based on one particular piece of
information in isolation. To decide whether you should
deliberately hold property through a limited company, you
need to consider all potential costs, all potential benefits (and the
likelihood of you enjoying them) and all potential risks.

The second reason people give for holding property inside a
limited company (and, this time, it is a trading company) is a
personal lack of funds. Sometimes, it is the company that has the
cash for the deposit and, in truth, at the time of the original
purchase, it was the only way of getting the lender on-side and
the property secured. All of the potential pros and cons
mentioned earlier apply here too, but there is one additional risk
I feel needs to be pointed out.

Certainly, in my own financial life, a move to investment
property ownership was a way of achieving two benefits:

♦ Much of my own wealth was attached to the success or
  otherwise of my business and I wanted to create a second
  stream of wealth creation that was not dependent upon
  that success.

♦ I recognised the relationship between the two major asset
  classes (property and equities) and how, typically, they
  moved in opposite directions, depending upon what stage
  of the economic cycle had been reached. A move to
  property was as much about introducing balance to my
  investment portfolio as a belief that now was the ideal time
  to invest.

If these risk management benefits are desirable to you, then recognise that holding a property on the balance sheet of your trading company achieves neither and, in fact, puts that property at greater risk. Belonging to the company, it is just another asset like the stock or the order book, and its retention into the future is completely dependent upon the commercial success of the business. If the business fails, the liquidator sells off your property to pay the creditors.

In many cases, historical financial circumstances led to the property being held within the company but, just because that is the way it was, does not mean it is the way it must always be. Let us look at an example to see whether this less than advantageous situation can be altered to the business owner's advantage. Assume an office/warehouse, like the ones situated in industrial estates that now seem to encircle nearly every sizeable town in Ireland. The property was purchased five years ago, by way of a 100%, 20-year capital and interest loan, for €300,000 and now has a value of €450,000. Based on an assumed interest rate of 5% *p.a.*, from the company's perspective, the cost of the loan over the next 15 years (the remaining term of the loan) will be:

	€
Monthly payment to lender	2,006.06
Average monthly corporation tax saving (@ 12.5%)*	94.51
Net monthly cost	1,911.55
Net cost over remaining 15-year term	**344,079.34**

* The corporation tax that is not paid, due to the interest deductions allowed within the company's accounts.

Having paid the loan for the past five years, the company still owes the lender €249,867.16 and will pay a further after-tax cost of €344,079.34 to repay this amount. If we assume the premises achieves a capital appreciation of 5% *p.a.* over the next 15 years, the building will be worth €1,193,984 once the loan is repaid.

If, once the loan is repaid, the business-owner decided to sell it and withdraw the cash, first the company will pay 20% CGT of *circa* €178,796 and then, assuming the business-owner can withdraw the money as capital, he/she will pay a further 20% CGT of *circa* €203,037 on the remaining cash. This is an effective tax rate of 42.7% on the gain of €893,984, or, put another way, the business-owner gets to keep only €812,151 of the sale proceeds.

Now, what if, having recognised the potential liabilities of the future, the business-owner decided to do something about it? He/she could buy the building now from the company at its current value of €450,000. The first cost to this transaction is the €30,000 in CGT the company will pay (20% of the €150,000 uplift between the original purchase price and the current value). The second cost is the stamp duty on the transfer, which will add a tax cost of €40,500 (9% of the €450,000*) to the structure.

Assume that the business-owner raises the €490,500 in a bank loan, to be repaid over the next 15 years. Having applied some of our new-found financial knowledge, we would structure the new loan on a retirement-backed basis, allowing the interest payments to be given to the business-owner by the company in the form of rent (which will be tax-free, as long as it is used to pay the bank interest) and the capital can be supplied by the company as a retirement contribution (which is also tax free in the business-owner's hands).

From the company's perspective, the costs will now be:

---

* I have not accounted for VAT in either calculation, as its payment makes no difference to the structuring example illustrated.

	€
Monthly rent	2,043.75
Lump sum payment to retirement fund *	196,800
Monthly regular contribution to retirement fund **	699
Average monthly tax saving (@ 12.5%)	342.84
Total net monthly outlay	2,399.91
Net cost over remaining 15-year term	**431,983.13**

* *At a sale price of €450,000, the company has received €226,821.14 more for the building than it owes the lender. Deducting the €30,000 CGT leaves it with surplus cash of €196,821.14 that can be invested in the business-owner's retirement plan immediately. These figures do not include the circa €24,600 in corporation tax rebate that the company can claim on this lump sum payment (always assuming that the company has trading profits against which to make such a claim), as the timing of any rebate will depend upon the business-owner's age and sex – his/her personal maximum allowances will dictate the timing of this rebate.*

** *As the business-owner will pay 'exit' tax and levies of 46% on 75% of the retirement fund on withdrawal, this monthly contribution, assuming an annual growth in the retirement fund of 6%, will grow to €687,025, which will net down to the required €450,000.*

So, you can see that, from a cash flow point of view, the company's outlay changes from a net €1,911.55 per month to €2,399.91 in our new example, a monthly increase of €488.36. The new process has cost an additional €87,905. However, in 15 year's time, keeping the 5% *p.a.* growth assumption, the building is worth €1,193,984, which the business-owner can sell and pay just one CGT liability of €148,797, keeping €1,045,187 after tax (€233,036 more than current structure will allow).

One way to view this planning intervention is to compare the additional cost (€158,405 – made up of an up-front cost of €70,500 and an additional monthly amount of €365.15 over the next 15 years) to the superior benefit (€233,036). The internal rate of return on this "investment" is 3.28% *p.a.*, a benefit secured for the business-owner by using the business' money, and one that could be considerably larger if the value rises faster than predicted in our calculation. The new owner of the building has increased his/her own wealth creation, simply by changing the way the property is held and the manner in which the loan is repaid.

As with each of the planning examples given in this chapter, I am not suggesting that such a result can be delivered in every case where a premises currently is held on the balance sheet of a trading company. The potential benefits will fall and rise, depending upon when the building was purchased, how much it has increased in value since purchase, what type (and what term) of loan is currently in place, when you plan to sell, etc. I present the example simply to demonstrate the kind of benefits that could accrue to a proprietary director in such circumstances, so that those proprietary directors reading this (or those who will become such directors in the future) at least will start to question whether a debt-structuring exercise is worthy of consideration. Put another way, "it ain't what you've done, but how it might be re-done" – everything is re-negotiable. It is certainly true in my day-to-day business life that, often, the greatest benefits delivered to our clients are delivered as we re-structure the financial past.

One of the most important financial disciplines you can impose on yourself is a regular review. While none of us possess a working crystal ball, we can predict quite confidently that tomorrow will be different from today. Our own personal circumstances change, the tax code changes regularly and the financial institutions and advisers are constantly coming up with new and innovative products and services. Despite the fact that we all know change to be an unavoidable part of modern life, few of us review historical financial decisions in the light of those changes. So, in our previous example, where a property ends up on the balance sheet of a company, because that was the only way the property could have been purchased back then, the decision must be reviewed as circumstances change.

6

WHY DIDN'T MY ACCOUNTANT
TELL ME ABOUT THIS?

The title for this chapter is shamelessly lifted directly from my experience of talking to clients and potential clients of *Financial Engineering Network Ltd*. Whether I am outlining some of the wealth creation and/or tax minimisation structures we use to one person or a group of people, this is often the first question I am asked.

But there is another question I am regularly asked that I want to share with you, along with my usual answer:

Question: *"Have you ever met an accountant who knows more about tax than you do?"*

Answer: *"Every accountant I have met knows more about tax than I do. However, I've never met one that knows more about not paying tax than I do!"*

I was asked this question, and gave this answer, at a seminar in Navan recently. I was followed onto the podium by a chartered accountant, who happened to agree with my answer. He told the audience: *"I spent seven years training to be a chartered accountant and, in that time, I was taught 430 ways to pay tax but not one single way of not paying tax."*

Before proceeding to answer the main question, I want to make it clear that there are accountancy firms that have specialist wealth management personnel on their staff and there are accountants who have specialist practices in tax or investment or pensions, but these are not the practices I am referring to here. As you will see later in this chapter, I believe that, very often, many who deal with accountancy firms that have no such expertise expect them to have it, despite the fact that the accountant has neither promised the service nor has levied a fee to provide such a service.

The truth of the matter is that, to run a compliant and successful business (from a wealth accumulation perspective), you need both sets of talents. To ensure you make all your tax payments on time, and thus keep yourself out of the courts (or, in a worst-case scenario, out of prison), you need someone who knows the tax payment rules and who ensures that you comply with them in a timely fashion. To maximise the wealth creation in your life, you need someone who knows how to legitimately minimise your tax liabilities. It is very rare indeed for one person (or even one firm) to possess both talents.

Returning now to the original question, in reality, there are only two possible answers to it:

♦ Your accountant does not know.

♦ Your accountant knows but, for some reason, has failed to tell you.

Let's deal with each answer in turn.

YOUR ACCOUNTANT DOES NOT KNOW

One of the common misconceptions amongst business owners is that accountants are all-knowing. As the accountant who followed me on stage in Navan admitted, this is certainly not the case. The financial services arena covers everything from banking to off-shore investments, from the production of compliant accounts to the selling of insurance. Your accountant, no more than any other professional within the financial services industry, is unlikely to have in-depth knowledge of all areas relevant to your entire financial life.

By now, you realise that **wealth accumulation** is a very different discipline from **income generation** and so requires specialist knowledge. In my experience, there are no more wealthy accountants in Ireland than there are wealthy people in any other profession. What this tells me is that the skills learned as one becomes an accountant give no apparent advantage towards creating and accumulating wealth.

A newly-qualified accountant is certainly more financially aware than most, but this awareness only stretches so far. He/she will know, in theory at least, all that is needed to perform the role of an accountant, but many of us assume that such knowledge stretches also to wealth accumulation tactics. While I have no doubt that there are accountants as well-versed, and even better-versed, as I am in the area of wealth creation (it's just that I have not met such an individual yet), they are likely to be the exception rather than the rule.

In truth, like so many of the obstacles that stand in the way of you accumulating wealth, the problem many perceive with their accountants is of their own making. Assuming anything (we all know) is inherently dangerous and I believe some of us assume our accountant's role is to help us avoid tax (legitimately) and to assist us in our efforts to create wealth. However, this is not the case, especially if we have never discussed this with our accountant and never agreed that it is part of the service we are seeking. As already stated, the primary role of your accountant is to ensure that you comply with Revenue rules and that you pay your taxes in a timely fashion. Any accountant who is involved in the preparation of your accounts and/or audits will see this as their core activity and it is unfair of you to expect anything more. We expect accountants to be tax consultants, investment intermediaries, pensions advisers and property gurus, but the vast majority of them are not! They have not promised these services and yet we expect them anyway and even get annoyed when they fail to live up to our own, unrealistic, expectations.

Advice on wealth creation has to come, may I suggest, from a source that has a proven track record in creating wealth. Therefore, first and foremost, one acid test as to whether your accountant is so qualified has to be his/her own wealth. Taking advice about becoming wealthy from someone (or some firm) that is neither wealthy, nor on the road to wealth, is akin to taking advice about your golf game from someone who has no record of being able to teach the sport and/or no qualifications to do so.

Indeed, this leads me to a point I want to make. If, for example, you want to improve your golf game, what do you do? You seek out a professional, pay him/her a fee to teach you new techniques and then practise those new techniques until your game improves. If you want to learn to play tennis, to improve your computer skills, to take on any new skills, that is what you do. We know this is the way to improve our own abilities – and yet we do not apply this same knowledge to the "skill" of wealth creation. We certainly would not accept golf lessons, and pay for them, from anyone who was not qualified to teach us and yet, in so many ways, we accept financial advice without checking the qualifications, relevant experience and track record of the adviser.

We have to recognise that, for the most part, we cannot change other people, we can only change ourselves. One such change, where the goal of true wealth creation is active in our world, is to be much more discerning about the source of the financial advice we receive. It may be worth re-reading **Chapter 1** to remind yourself of how to choose a financial adviser.

YOUR ACCOUNTANT KNOWS, BUT HAS FAILED TO TELL YOU

In my view, there are also only two possible explanations here. The first returns to my comments made in the previous section, in that it may be because your accountant does not believe it to be his/her job to impart such knowledge. Despite the fact that, for the most part, our accountants only promise to produce our accounts or carry out audits, we still assume they are there to do much more. In truth, our accountants neither promised this service nor are being paid to provide it and so our expectations are unrealistic.

Secondly, and I admit this is a more cynical suggestion, the fact that some accountants choose not to be authorised to deliver audits may be a contributor. For example, if your accountant has not been authorised to audit limited companies and you are currently operating as a sole trader, then suggesting you should operate as a limited company would be the same as telling you to find another accountant. So, in such an environment, despite the considerable advantages you may enjoy as the owner of limited company, this could be the reason you are not told.

Without knowing your current financial circumstances and details of your relationship with your accountant, it is, of course, impossible for me to answer the question posed in this chapter's title. This said, there are certainly some changes you can make to the way you interact with your accountant (and other financial advisers) that will improve your own financial life.

ALWAYS GET ADVICE IN WRITING

The Financial Regulator clearly states that, if any financial advice you receive is not in writing, then "it does not exist". While most of us insist on written confirmation from banks, insurance salesmen etc, many of us do not make the same demands of our accountants. Perhaps it is familiarity, or just a bad habit we have developed over time but, in the search for well thought-out, professional and expert advice around wealth accumulation, it is a habit we need to break.

Some reading this will interpret this suggestion as one that indicates a lack of trust and may even feel that asking for advice in writing would be a veiled insult to their accountant. I am certainly not attempting in any way to discredit your accountant and you will not be doing so, if you demand written advice. However, my personal experience, as I have stated already, is that accountants themselves contribute to our misunderstanding of their core expertise. Despite having little or no training or experience in such matters, I have found many, but admittedly not all, accountants willing to offer verbal advice on everything from syndicated property investments to self-administered retirement trusts, and from the arrangement of leasing finance to the retirement backing of long-term investment debt.

Recognising that you need better information in order to make better financial decisions has nothing to do with trust, and demanding that such information is imparted in writing is just one of the changes you are making to your financial world. Whether there is a real need to change your financial world is only something you can decide, but the very fact that you are reading this book suggests that, at least, you are open to the possibility. If the way you have received financial advice from your accountant (or other financial advisers) has always meant that you have made the right financial decision at the right time, then there is no need to change a thing. However, if you are not sure that your historical decisions were – and remain – correct, then something needs to change. Otherwise, nothing will change.

QUESTION ALL ADVICE UNTIL YOU ARE SURE THAT IT IS RIGHT FOR YOU

I have met people in my professional life who unquestioningly follow their accountant's advice. In my business, we tell prospective clients that we will not be making their financial decisions for them, but that we will be giving them improved, and more in-depth, information so that they can make better financial decisions for themselves. This is because we firmly believe that only when you take responsibility for your own money will the necessary changes occur (to make wealth accumulation an integral part of your financial world). We all have a tendency to abdicate responsibility for our financial decisions, preferring in many cases to let others make the decisions, perhaps because we can blame them if things do not go as planned? Of course, many of us do this with the justification: *"Well, I know nothing about this kind of thing"*. This, in my opinion, is one of the obstacles that stands in the way of us all enjoying the best financial results possible from our current financial circumstances.

From now on, you need to understand fully every financial action you are to take (or to understand fully why you are not taking a particular action). The only way you can achieve this is by asking questions. Never be embarrassed by your lack of knowledge and never be afraid to say you do not understand. Your advisers are supposed to be able to impart their expertise to you in a manner that you do understand. If something is explained to you (or if you receive an answer to one of your questions) and you still do not understand, that is the adviser's problem, not yours! I suggest that the reason you do not understand is because it is not being explained to you properly and not because you are too foolish or too ignorant. I have witnessed many people make a decision to invest, or a decision not to invest, to save themselves the emotional trauma of having to admit that they do not understand. They may save themselves some discomfort by playing the *"Well, I know nothing about this sort of thing but if you (the accountant in this example, but similar comments are made to bank managers, insurance brokers, etc) say it's OK, then I am fine with that"* card but, if such a practice has not led them to true wealth creation, then I have no hesitation in suggesting they abandon the practice immediately.

I stated at the start of this chapter that, in effect, there are only two possible answers to the question posed in the title. I also stated at the very start of this book that wealth creation has much more to do with the **way** you run your financial world than the investments you make. The same may well be true about how you deal with, and what you expect from, your accountant. Although one cannot generalise too much, in my experience the vast majority of us expect too much from the men and women of the accountancy profession. Also, it is my experience that the vast majority of us take our accountant's advice with little or no questioning. Neither practice is fully compatible with true wealth creation.

Finally, while I am generalising here, it would be unfair of me not to state that I am aware of accountants who are very different to the norm (and, therefore, fully concede that particular readers may well disagree with much of my generalisations). So, accountants do exist who have far more to offer than the basics, who have created real wealth for themselves and have the ability to advise on the topic, who have specialist tax and/or investment experts on their staff.

I have met clients of such accountants who, through no fault of the accountants, have failed to take advantage of the opportunities their adviser could provide. Invariably, when I come across this scenario, it is the clients who are to blame. Despite their accountant's best intentions and demonstrable skills, these clients are the ones who deliver their papers to their accountant an hour before the tax filing deadline. Yet these same people are still miffed that their accountant could not save them some tax. No matter what the expertise or experience of any financial adviser, may I suggest that only someone with truly magical powers could help you if you give them just an hour (or just a day or even just a week) in which to work.

7

NEITHER A BORROWER NOR A LENDER BE

The great Bard wrote the tragedy of *Hamlet* in 1592. The title of this chapter is taken from a scene where a father is offering advice to his son, before the son embarks on a long journey. Not only was it well-meaning but, back in 1592, it was also excellent advice as, for example, failing to repay your debts could result in a swift introduction to the working end of a sword.

Despite being written over four centuries ago, I am amazed by how many people continue to live their lives by this mantra. Again, may I suggest that whoever first introduced them to this advice was well-meaning but, unlike in 1592, debt is no longer a matter of life and death. In my view, if you desire to create wealth and are unwilling to borrow money to make investments, then you are quite simply making your financial goals infinitely more difficult to achieve. I would liken it to setting off to run a marathon with your shoe-laces tied together. While it is possible to complete the race, it would be impossible to do so in any reasonable time and the most likely outcome is that you would grind to a halt somewhere along the course and give up.

To most of us, when we hear this mantra, what we really hear is "don't borrow money", but, of course, it also says "don't lend money". If you need proof that the message is outdated and relatively useless in the 21st-century world, take a look at the value of the financial institutions that lend money. In Ireland, the most valuable public companies quoted on our stock market are those involved, generally as their core business, in lending money.

Returning for a moment to the concerned father's advice in *Hamlet*, for the time, he was correct and offered his advice to keep the son he loved safe. However, a father offering the same advice in 2007 is actually undermining his son's ambitions (if wealth accumulation is his son's ultimate goal), despite the fact that it may be offered with the same love and concern that Shakespeare's character showed for his son.

To use the title of my previous book, one of the real *Tricks of the Rich* is that, once they create a little wealth, they borrow against it to create some more. You have heard the phrase "money makes money"? In reality, the extended version of this is "having some money allows you to borrow some more and investing the borrowings creates more money" – it just does not roll off the tongue as easily as the shortened version.

Debt can be defined as either "good debt" or "bad debt" and, to avoid any confusion, in this chapter, of course, I am referring to the "good" type. Good debt is where the debt is raised to make an investment that has the potential to make you wealthier; bad debt is generally debt raised to purchase a consumable, where there is no possibility of you getting wealthier. Where good debt is concerned, the following statement is true:

"As long as the return on the investment you make with borrowed money is greater than the cost of the debt, you are making money for free!"

The way you repay investment debt contributes hugely to the true costs and, obviously, the lower the effective cost of any such debt, the more likely you are to enjoy an investment return in excess of those costs. Judging the likelihood of any particular investment to outperform the cost of your debt is how you go about judging the risk being taken. Indeed, may I suggest that, if you are a person who has held the view that being debt-free is a positive financial position, it is because you perceive the risks of debt to be too great. May I go even further and suggest that it is a fear of the risks that keeps you focused on having as little debt as possible.

RISK

Risk is like anything in life that causes you to feel the fear emotion. The fear itself generally comes from a lack of familiarity and/or understanding. As children, we fear the dark, we fear certain animals, we fear heights and large bodies of water but, as our familiarity with, and understanding of, these things grow, our fear dissipates and, for most of us, all but disappears altogether. The fear emotion is a paralysing one, for all sentient beings that inhabit this planet. Making financial decisions with your emotions (the other active emotion being greed) is not the way to create wealth. Realise now that, just as your childhood fears disappeared as your knowledge of the world around you and your own personal skills grew (for example, the fear of large bodies of water may have disappeared when you learned to swim), so too will your fear of risk disappear when you understand it better and when your knowledge grows to allow you to judge, unemotionally, investment risk for yourself.

By way of example, let us examine the fears one may encounter when buying an investment property (with borrowings). The following are the fears you may have to deal with, along with some comments designed to demonstrate that the risks may not be as great as you believe. Recognise too that, in the real world, "people's perceptions are their own reality" (I cannot remember where I first read this quote) and, for you, the reality of risk will change, only if you change the way you perceive it.

Interest Rates May Rise

Obviously, when borrowing, for any purchase, on a variable rate (one that changes as market interest rates rise and fall), there is the potential for the cost of the loan to rise. One method you can use to give yourself some idea of what will happen to interest rates in the near future is to ask your lender to tell you the fixed rates over the next two, three, or even five years. If these rates are higher than the current variable rates, then you can be fairly sure that your lender believes that interest rates will rise in the future. If such rates are lower, then the opposite can be deduced.

So, rather than simply failing to act because of your (uninformed) fear, why not ask the question and see whether your perception of rising interest rates is shared by your financial institution (which, may I add, is probably in a much better position to judge where interest rates are going than you are).

Even if rates are expected to rise, this does not automatically mean you should avoid borrowing. Instead, run your numbers on the property, assuming the highest interest rate you have been quoted, and see whether you can still create wealth, even in that worst-case scenario. Doing this – and yet still borrowing on a variable rate – means that, even if rates rise to their predicted maximum, you have convinced yourself, before the investment is made, that you can handle the costs.

Alternatively, you could choose to arrange your finance on a fixed rate basis, which will mean that, for the duration of the fixed period at least, no matter what happens to interest rates, your costs will stay constant.

The Property May De-value

Again, it is perfectly possible that, for example, in a short-term rising interest rate environment, a property's value could decrease. However, remember that true wealth creation happens *over the long term*. I find it impossible to contemplate an environment where property bought today would be generally less valuable in, say, 10, 15 or 20 years' time. This is not to say that I cannot imagine such an environment, but it would require a catastrophic economic event or a series of such catastrophic events. While that is possible, it is improbable in my opinion and, to be frank, in the event of such catastrophe, I imagine the last thing on my mind will be the value of my investment property! For this to happen, the Western world would have to be on its knees and we would be more worried about the air we breathe and/or having enough food to eat (for example, in the event of a large-scale nuclear war).

When buying such a property, the short-term capital gain or loss is irrelevant; much more important is judging the letting potential and thus deciding how much of your own money will you be required to part with on an ongoing basis. Here, may I repeat some suggestions made in my previous book on selecting a residential investment property:

♦ In order to gauge what area will produce the most demand from potential tenants, place a number of "dummy" advertisements in the newspapers, offering the type of property you are considering buying in a number of different residential areas, as if you had already bought. Give a phone number with a voice-mail (so that you do not have to deal personally with the enquiries) and, after a while, count the number of enquiries in each location. This will cost you a few euro (but not much) and will immediately tell you where the letting demand is highest.

♦ Run your numbers based on a 10-month letting period each year and at the lowest rent that you have been told such a property will demand. In this way, you are making your decision based on, within reason, a worst-case scenario and any post-purchase 'surprises' on finance should be positive.

I would like to add a third suggestion to the ones made in the previous book and that is to visit an independent letting agent in the location you are considering. Independent letting agents are not involved in property sales and make all of their income by letting other people's property. This means that they are less inclined to talk up a particular property (which could happen if the letting agent is part of the same organisation that is offering the property for sale). Letting agents only want properties on their books that they can let and, therefore, are a good source of advice for the investor, since they are unlikely to tell you to buy a property that they could not let and could not make money from.

The Tenants May Default on Their Rent

This is potentially a problem for any landlord but one that can be managed by using a letting agent to handle your property. The agents will reduce this risk, as they will demand references from any potential tenant. While this will add a layer of cost to the transaction (I personally pay my Irish letting agent 10% of the rental income I receive), it will massively reduce the 'hassle factor' of being a landlord, as well as reducing the risks.

No amount of preparation for any investment you care to consider will eliminate altogether the risks of fraud but the more rigorous the checks you put your tenants through, the more you will weed out potential "bad" tenants.

The Maintenance/Refurbishment Costs Might Ruin My Investment

While, from time to time, you will incur unexpected costs (leaking pipes, painting and decorating, etc), you can reduce the risk by being diligent as you buy the property and by being prudent when running your financial numbers.

For the former, hiring a qualified surveyor to give the house a once-over before you buy will tell you a lot. It will cost some money but the fee is likely to be less than one-quarter of one percent of the purchase price.

For ongoing maintenance, when you do your numbers, set aside around 10% *p.a.* of the annual rent to cover these costs and make sure you can still afford it, based on this assumption. Finally, recognise that such costs are legitimate expenses for any landlord and can be paid out of your rental income before tax is paid. Based on a top tax take of 46% (41% tax and 5% levies), the real cost to you is only 54% of the actual costs (in other words, these costs will only be around half of what you expect them to be).

Remember too, the lessons you learned in **Chapter 3**, in that you are likely to have a loan repayment structure that suits you (and not just the lender), which is estimated to reduce the real cost of your loan (when compared to those who simply accept the bank's "advice") by between 10% and 30%, possibly more. Integrating your new knowledge on debt into your decision-making process allows you to be more enthusiastic about a particular project than the investor who has to pay considerably more for the property.

Fear is an inevitable part of attempting to create wealth, no matter who you are or what your background. Every investor feels fear to a greater or lesser extent, so fear itself is not the problem. The problems are created by how we deal with the fear: some let it paralyse them and thus do nothing; others educate themselves, understand the risks and accept them, based on the potential rewards. It is not that they do not feel the fear, although their superior knowledge lessens its intensity, but they simply "feel the fear and do it anyway".

It may surprise you that, if you have the cash available for a particular investment, my suggestion is that you borrow the money! This suggestion is made based on the assumption that the investment to be made is "allowable for tax purposes" and thus you will receive a tax deduction against your interest payments.

Let us look at an example, again using an investment property purchase, to illustrate the benefits. Let's assume you wish to buy a residential property for letting at a price of €400,000 (inclusive of all fees and levies). You have the cash and decide to use it. Based on a rental yield of 3% *p.a.*, assumed to be received for an average of 10 months each year, the following is the income you will receive and the taxes you will pay:

	€
Monthly rental income	833.33
Income tax (41%) + levies (5%) *	383.33
Net rental income	**450.00**

*   *Assuming normal tax credits are used against other income.*

You get to keep €450 a month, based on our assumptions.

Now let's look at an alternative structure. This time, you will place your €400,000 cash on long-term deposit and will borrow the money to purchase the property, on an interest-only basis (you have no need to repay the capital, as this can be done at any time from the deposit). Assuming you get a gross 4% *p.a.* from the deposit account, the following will be your monthly income from the cash:

	€
Gross monthly income	1,333,33
DIRT (20%)	266.67
Net monthly income	1,066.66

Now, borrowing the money will mean monthly servicing costs and assuming a 4% *p.a.* interest rate on the debt (you can assume a low cost of finance here, as the lender has no security risk whatsoever), this will cost you €1,333.33 per month. However, the fact that you pay this interest means you pay no tax on your rental income. You get to keep it all. Thus, the overall financial position now looks like this:

	€
Net monthly deposit income	1,066.66
Net monthly rental income	833.33
Less cost of finance	(1,333.33)
Net income	**566.60**

So, simply by changing the **way** you do things, this time to take advantage of the low deposit interest retention tax (DIRT) and the tax deductibility of interest payments on investment debt, you have increased your after-tax income by €116.60 per month or by 25.9%.

In my experience, debt, like risk, is viewed by most people in a very black-and-white manner. Most assume that more debt means more cost and less income in their pocket but, as the last example proves, this is simply not the case. At the very beginning of this book, I said that I would challenge your beliefs around money and thus challenge you to think more deeply about your financial actions. If you have viewed all debt in a negative manner, if you have voiced the ambition to be debt-free, then perhaps you need to revisit your attitudes and beliefs?

PROPERTY *vs* EQUITIES

One of the long-running debates in the financial world has been property *vs* equities and which investment type has the greater potential. In truth, in the last decade or so, most Irish investors have made more money in property than the stock markets, but not because property has risen in value at a faster pace! The reason for the greater wealth creation is that investors have been able to make their investment, in part, if not in total, with other people's money (the lender's) and to also repay the debt (in part, if not in total) with someone else's money (the tenant's). So it is the **way** these investors made the investment (and the **way** they repaid the debt) that, in effect, has bolted a "turbo-charger" onto the investment "vehicle".

On a straight cash investment, over any longer term period you care to mention, the equity markets actually have outperformed the property markets. This is not to say that one could not find an exception to this "rule"; it is perfectly possible to find a particular property investment that outperformed a specific equity alternative over a given period of time. However, from an overall market perspective, even when the meteoric rise in Irish residential property value over the last two decades is taken into account, equities have outperformed property!

Indeed, if you think about it for a moment, this truth should not surprise you as, quite frankly, it is hard to imagine a property boom that would not be contributed to by an equity boom. Most people who buy a new house, who trade up to a bigger house or who invest in a residential property for letting purposes, can only do so if they have a good job. If they have a good job that pays them well, that is only sustained if their employer is doing well and making and growing profit. If employers are doing well and growing their profits, their value is growing and thus the stock markets are growing too. Everything is linked.

In our business, we have long recognised the wealth our clients can create by using other people's money and have always dreamed of being able to use borrowing to increase exponentially the returns from the stock markets. The problem has been that lenders have not been too happy to lend to investors in the stock market. Even those who have provided loans for such investments have limited the amount of finance they provide, with the highest loan-to-value (LTV) I have seen being 50% (whereas property investors typically receive 75% to 95% finance) – and one could not fault them for that. They are in the business of managing their own risk (not yours) and, other than property in the immediate vicinity of a disaster, it is hard to imagine a property (over which they take a lien to back the loan) dropping in value by, say, 40% in a day. It is not quite so hard to imagine an equity dropping in value by such an amount in a day – indeed, there are very many historical examples of such devaluations.

To take a brief aside for a moment, I am reminded of a debate that took place in Dublin a number of years ago. The topic of property *vs* equities was being debated, with property represented by a spokesperson from one of Ireland's top auctioneering firms and equities by a gentleman from one of our major banks. As the protagonists finished their prepared presentations, the "equities" argument was winning the day, but victory was dampened somewhat by a question from the audience, posed to the banker: *"If equities are so good, why will your employer not lend money for us to buy them? It will not even lend for us to buy your own shares!"*

The poor banker was less than prepared for this question. He had spent his allotted time deftly proving that, over any reasonably lengthy period, equities outperformed the property market. However, much of his credibility evaporated, as he floundered.

I cannot say why he floundered, since the answer is actually quite simple: in my view, his employer was unwilling to accept the risk. A lender has two main concerns when lending money:

- The borrower must demonstrate an ability to repay the loan.

- The borrower must provide adequate security so that, in the event of a failure to make the repayments, the lender has a legal entitlement to sell the secured asset and get its money back.

While the banker in our story convinced himself and his audience that, over any reasonable time (and in the absence of an economic catastrophe of World War-like proportions), the equity markets will continue to outperform all other assets, his employer was not willing to take the risks involved in lending for the purchase of equities. In the event of a default on the part of a borrower, the bank could find itself in double jeopardy, with a defaulting borrower and a secured asset that had, albeit in the short-term, fallen in value. Ironically, due to the more stable values enjoyed by a property, the bank would be more happy to lend, even for the borrower to invest in equities, if a property was provided as the security.

The point of all this is that it is not the absence of long-term potential in equities that has scared banks away from lending to investors in that market; it is the volatility of the value of the asset that frightens them. Banks, the vast majority of which also are involved in equity fund management, are well aware of the potential of these assets to outperform, but that awareness does not mean they want to risk their lending organisations. Lenders, no more than bookmakers, are not involved in the risk business – they make very fine profits on a tried and tested, virtually risk-free, business model. Of course, there are times when a particular deal for a lender (or a particular bet for a bookmaker, I imagine) in isolation may be viewed as a risk but, overall, once they stick to their operational rules, the lender (or the bookmaker) is guaranteed to make money.

It was certainly frustrating, as a financial adviser, not to be able to link up the "turbo-charger" (of making investments with other people's money) to the equity investment vehicle. We always knew that, if it were possible, the wealth creation outcome could be spectacular. I am glad to report that, in recent times, this has been made possible with the introduction of what are known as "geared trackers".

The humble tracker bond has been around for many years and, despite much of the press and media coverage, is a relatively simple product. A typical tracker bond, which always has a fixed term (three, five, six years, etc), is really two products in one:

♦ A certain amount of the money invested is placed on deposit and is guaranteed to grow back, over the product term, to the amount originally invested. The higher the interest rate available from the product provider, the lower the amount of money that has to be invested in the deposit element of the product. For example, imagine investing €100,000 into a tracker over six years. If the net of tax return available from the deposit provider was a guaranteed 3% *p.a.*, then €83,748.43 of the €100,000 investment would be placed on deposit. If the deposit interest rate after tax was guaranteed to deliver 4% *p.a.*, then only €79,031.45 of the €100,000 investment would be needed on deposit. In both examples, based on the assumed net interest rate, each amount would mature at a value of €100,000 after six years.

♦ Having effectively underwritten the capital guarantee
within the deposit account, the product manufacturer now
has between €20,968.55 (€100,000 less €79,031.45) and
€16,251.57 (€100,000 less €83,748.43) of the investor's
money remaining. With this money, the product
manufacturer purchases an option on the equity index to
be tracked (this could be a market index, such as the Dow
Jones, FTSE-100 or ISEQ, or a sector index, such as
European pharmaceuticals, American financials or
Japanese property stocks) and the participation rate will be
dependent upon the option provider's view of the market
chosen. An option, again despite many people's belief, is a
relatively simple concept. Assuming the higher number of
€20,968.55 in the example, what the product manufacturer
wants to know is how much this figure can buy in the
index/indices chosen – this will dictate the tracker's
"participation rate". The €20,968.55 will be paid
immediately to the option provider, who will promise to
sell a certain amount of the index being tracked, at today's
price (or to be exact at the price on the "strike date" of the
tracker, the effective start date of the six-year term in this
example). So, to get a participation rate of 100%, the
€20,968.55 would have to secure €100,000 worth of the
index, at today's price, six years from now.

♦ The two elements come together at the end of the tracker
period. In the event that the index is more valuable in six
years' time than it was on the start date, then the option
will be exercised and profit will be made. In this example,
let us assume that the index being tracked (for simplicity of
explanation) is valued at 1,000 on the start date and has
grown to 2,000 in the six years. As the deposit account
matures (at €100,000) within the tracker, under the terms
of the option, that €100,000 can buy the index at 1,000 and
immediately sell it the same day at 2,000, doubling the
money in a day and repaying the investor €200,000 as a

maturity value. However, in the event that the index being tracked has fallen in value to, say, 750, over the six years, then the option is useless and the investor only receives the €100,000 back. In effect, the €20,968.55 paid to the option provider has been completely lost and, in effect, has been replaced in the investor's hands by the guaranteed returns on the deposit element.

OK, that might not be as simple as I predicted, but I hope that, even if it means reading it a couple of times, you get the broad picture. A tracker uses two financial products bolted together to allow an investor to get the potential returns offered by the stock market, while having a guarantee on the capital invested.

The fact that a capital guarantee was introduced by the tracker products opened the door to investors to borrow the money to invest. In the previous example, the investor could happily borrow the €100,000 and invest in the tracker, as he/she is guaranteed to get the €100,000 back in six years' time and thus is guaranteed to be able to repay the amount borrowed at the end of the loan term. He/she could offer the tracker as security to the lender. This means that, from a financial underwriting point of view, the lender has a 100% guarantee on the capital. Thus its only concern when underwriting the investor's loan application is his/her ability to service the interest payments. Indeed, from the investor's point of view, the monthly interest payments are his/her only concern too and, in the example, his/her only risk!

Assuming, for example, no growth whatsoever in the index being tracked, at the end of six years the maximum loss the investor could suffer is the interest payments made over the six years.

Let's look at some figures. First, look at a straight €100,000 cash investment in a tracker, which offers a 100% participation rate on an index that produces a 6% *p.a.* growth over the six-year investment, *via* the method demonstrated earlier. The future maturity value of this product is: **€141,851.91**.

Depending upon your own tax status and the design of the product itself (some are categorised as deposit accounts and liable to DIRT – some investors can be exempt from DIRT and all retirement funds are so exempt – and some products are categorised as life insurance policies that are liable to exit tax), tax may be payable on this maturity value but, for the purposes of this illustration, I want to ignore tax. Whether you invest your own cash or money borrowed from a lender, the tax treatment of profits will be exactly the same. Thus, it is not relevant when attempting to demonstrate the difference in wealth creation between investing cash or borrowed funds.

So, in the example, the investor has received a 6% *p.a.* return. Now assume that the €100,000 was borrowed and the investor paid an annual interest rate of 4.5%. The monthly, interest-only payment (there is no need to repay the capital, as this is guaranteed to be repaid by the tracker itself), is **€375**.

For his/her investment of €375 per month, keeping with our 6% *p.a.* growth assumption, he/she will receive the following return: €41,851.91 (the maturity value of the tracker less the repayment of the €100,000 loan).

The annual return for the investor has risen from 6% *p.a.* to 13.59% – the manner in which the investment is undertaken has more than doubled the effective yield.

Of course, to get this more than double return, the investor has had to take on additional risk. In a straight cash investment, the only risk being taken is the returns he/she would have received had the €100,000 been placed within a guaranteed type product such as a deposit account. In the geared (loan) example, the risk being taken is the €375 per month over 72 months, a total of €28,125 (and which could rise if interest rates rise), all of which could be lost.

Of course, in and of itself, identifying the sum at risk (the €28,125) is less than helpful, since one has to examine the potential for this loss to be suffered. Back-testing the index being tracked over a number of differing six-year timeframes (and, if you wish, such back-testing could be done for every six-year period in the index's history) will tell you what the real likelihood of suffering a real loss will be.

For example, in the borrowing example, the index needs to produce a return of 4.14% *p.a.* for our investor to break-even. If this was achieved, the maturity value of the tracker would be €128,125, thus repaying the loan and also refunding the total interest payments. For the investor to make a profit, therefore, the index has to produce 4.15% *p.a.* or more and the back-testing should tell you the likelihood of this performance.

I suggest that, whether you look at many different six-year timeframes or just a couple, your back-testing should include a period where the stock markets performed particularly badly. For example, between 2000 and 2003, the markets had their worst-ever long-term decline (heavily contributed to by the dot-com collapse) and including this period in a six-year back-test would demonstrate to you one of the worst outcomes one could realistically predict. The crash of 1987 ("Black Monday"), the oil crisis of 1973-74, or even the 1929 collapse (some of the earlier examples may not be helpful if the index to be tracked post-dates these events) can, and should, be included in your back-testing.

Unfortunately, as I write this section, due to less than positive media attention, the future of these geared trackers seems at risk. What is, in my opinion, more unfortunate is that the problem with these products is not the product itself but the manner in which it has been sold. Journalists involved, rightly so in my view, have called into question some of the sales tactics used and have received complaints from people who invested with unrealistic expectations and without fully understanding the risks. One could say they made their investment decision without knowing the full costs, benefits and risks and it will not surprise you that such a decision-making process can lead, in many cases, to the wrong choice being made. People, it would seem, borrowed without understanding that their interest costs could rise (a risk that can be removed by fixing the interest rate) and this is the last risk you need to consider before making your final decision.

Whether the packaged product continues to be available or not, you will be able to avail of this type of planning regardless, as long as trackers survive. The borrowing and investment do not have to be arranged within one product, since you can do them separately. Indeed, for those investors with even more appetite for risk, the direct purchase of an option in isolation could do exactly the same thing (projected returns could be even greater, as could potential losses) but I feel it is beyond the remit of this volume to delve deeply into such specialist investments, as the weight of money needed to 'self-manufacture' in this manner would be beyond all but an elite few (and those wealthy enough are probably doing it already).

The final issue you will have to take into consideration before you make such an investment is the terms and conditions of the tracker itself. Another complaint registered by recent media coverage revolves around the internal charges being levied within such products. While it is not usually, or immediately, obvious what those charges are, they are reflected in the terms you will be offered. Watch out for the "participation rate", which in the earlier example I assumed to be 100% (that is, your investment will get all of the growth delivered by the index). The participation rate can be higher or lower than 100% and, depending upon which you are being offered, can mean:

♦ **If lower:** A considerable part of your initial investment never reaches the investment itself. While, in the earlier illustration, the participation rate was assumed at 100%, you can imagine that if 10% of your investment disappeared in initial charges, then only €90,000 of your €100,000 would reach the investment. The same amount (€83,748.43, which we assumed using a deposit-based return of 3% *p.a.*) will have to be placed on deposit to grow back to €100,000 in six years, leaving just €6,251.57 (€90,000 less €83,748.43) available to purchase the option.

♦ **If higher:** If you are offered a participation rate higher than 100%, this may mean the index (or one of the indices, if a group of indices is being tracked) being tracked has a poor performance history and/or is expected to deliver poor performance. As you can imagine, it is easier for the option provider to offer a superior participation rate if their belief is that the option will not be exercised at the end (because the index value has fallen), in which case the investor only gets his/her money back from the guaranteed maturity of the deposit account.

In summary, borrowing to create wealth is generally a good idea and is certainly one of the "tricks of the rich". The main reasons are:

♦ You put yourself in the way of making money with other people's money.

♦ As long as the return on the investment is greater than the cost of your debt, you are making money for free!

♦ While there are risks, it is quite likely that they are far less than you perceive them to be and you should not let fear control your decision-making process.

♦ Many of the risks can be lowered by prudent planning. Making such investments inside a private retirement fund means that the true cost of the debt can be reduced by up to 46% (41% tax and 5% levies). Fixing interest rates can remove the risk of rising costs of debt. Full and proper back-testing will help and may prove that, other than in a catastrophic economic environment, it is all but impossible for you not to make money.

♦ Releasing equity from existing property assets through borrowing, not only allows you to bolt on a "turbo-charger" to your investment portfolio, but also can reduce

most people's serious over-exposure to property itself
(and, in so doing, reduce overall risk).

♦ Finally, you are likely to have enjoyed considerable wealth
creation through this method before, without necessarily
thinking about it. Many home-owners in Ireland have
experienced massive increases in their property values on
homes they bought with 90%+ gearing attached. I suggest
that the vast bulk of the wealth created has been due to the
debt (because you personally did not have to stump up the
cash to buy your house), considerably more than was
created by the property.

8
PLAN FOR THE NEXT GENERATION

I am firmly of the belief that you should always take care of the current generation before you start to make plans for the one to come. Thus, in my view, planning succession should take a back seat to planning your own financial freedom. Once your own financial future is secured, then you have both the time and the focus to apply to a properly-structured succession plan.

Many people I meet in my professional life almost wince when I mention succession – and who can blame them? None of us are comfortable with contemplating our own death. Also, in my experience, many of us believe that the succession of one's assets is a relatively straightforward exercise and that, other than making a will, and perhaps buying a life insurance policy to fund the tax liabilities of our heirs, there is little we can do to interfere with (and improve) the process. Others I have met take the following attitude: *"My parents left me with nothing. My kids will be far better off than I was. Let them pay the tax."*

Throughout this book, I have cautioned against making financial decisions without the full facts (without knowing all costs, benefits and risks) and I will sing the same song here too. If you are someone who would contribute to this train of thought, or simply someone who believes inheritance tax to be the only issue in succession planning, then the following issues may change your mind.

SUCCESSION ISSUES

You Need a Will, Even If Your Circumstances Are Relatively Simple

You have to realise that, if you have not written down your wishes in a formal will, and you die, then the State (*via* the Succession Act, 1965) will decide what happens to your estate. When our personal circumstances are "simple", which generally means your wishes are for your spouse to inherit your assets, and for your children to do so, many believe no action needs to be taken.

But, if you die intestate (without a will), the Succession Act (in a family circumstance) will give your spouse two-thirds of your estate and your children the other one-third, evenly divided. This may cause your spouse problems, especially, although not exclusively, if your children are very young, and could mean the survivors are unable to freely use the assets you leave behind.

Your Wishes Can Be Overturned in the Courts

Many people believe that the writing down of their wishes in a formal will guarantees that those wishes will be carried out. However, this is simply not always the case! Under the terms of the Succession Act 1965, any beneficiary (children being the people most protected by the succession laws in Ireland), who believes they have not been fairly treated, has a right to challenge any will and, in many cases, can have the will overturned.

Inheritance Tax and/or the Rate at which It Is Payable Is Not Inevitable

Many people are unaware of the planning opportunities that exist to reduce and, in some cases, eliminate altogether, the inheritance tax payable by your heirs. They are operating under a false impression, as you will see later in this chapter.

Other Influences May Decrease the Value of Your Estate by considerably more than a 20% Capital Acquisitions Tax Rate

Capital Acquisitions Tax (CAT) (payable by the recipient on the value of the amount, either inherited or received as a gift) is due in cash and within four months of the valuation date of inheritance (or gift). The valuation date can be as early as the date the donor died or as late as when the legalities of the estate have been finalised. Failure to pay the liabilities promptly will attract substantial financial penalties, with penalty interest levied at the rate of *circa* 10% *p.a.*

What this means is that recipients, unless they have substantial assets in their own right, are under considerable pressure to pay inheritance tax. This can lead to a quick sale of assets to fund the tax and to avoid the inevitable penalties. The vast bulk of inheritances (in Ireland, at least, but I would imagine the experience is repeated in most Western economies) are not in cash but in illiquid property assets and the need for a quick sale (or the news of a testate sale) becomes market gossip.

When you know the vendor requires cash quickly (and delay will cost them greatly in penalties), as a buyer, you seek to take advantage and offer less than you would normally. I have seen many estates suffer this "forced sale" problem and thus lose not only substantial value in the tax payable, but sometimes lose even greater value as people with cash take advantage of the cashless position of the beneficiaries. If this happened to your heirs, a considerably greater part of your estate (of your life's work, as it were) simply evaporates. Revenue may not take account of the fact that your heirs have to sell at lower than market rates and thus it is not even guaranteed that the forced sale, at less than market value, will lower the Revenue's tax computation (they can take the view that, just because you planned your estate badly, doesn't change the value, but simply lowers how much your heirs get to keep).

Debt Can Force the Sale of Inherited Assets

Assets can pass from one generation to another with debt attaching (principally property). What has to be considered here is whether the lenders will wish to continue to support the debt after your death. While a lender may have been more than happy to loan you money, they may not be happy to support your heirs in the same way. Often, the income of one's heirs (and income is how a lender judges ability to repay) is considerably lower than your own and this may cause the lender to call for the prompt repayment of the debt. This has the same potential to erode value as outlined in the previous section and may be a reason to cover all debt with life insurance, even if the lender does not demand that security.

The Inexperience of Heirs Can Erode Value

While you may be well used to dealing with the levels of wealth you leave behind, your heirs may not share that experience. This can leave them open to being taken advantage of by more experienced individuals and the requirement of the quick cash to repay debt simply increases the chances of this happening. Just as, through the purchase, and reading, of this book, if nothing else, you are attempting to increase your own financial knowledge, the sooner you can offer that experience and learning to your heirs, the better.

The Value of Your Assets May Not Survive Your Death

A particular problem that affects heirs of shares in private limited companies is that a private company wholly-owned (or effectively controlled) by one individual may have much of its real value vested in the individual himself/herself. This could mean your heirs paying substantial tax on an asset that, while correctly valued at the date of death, plummets in value once your heirs take control. Minority stakes in private companies, in general, are really only worth what the majority stakeholders are willing to pay and, without some form of legally binding valuation process, your heirs' inheritance is, at best, dependent upon the goodwill of others.

One or more of these issues may apply to your financial world and, if they do, then a properly structured succession plan is needed. But, before going into some of the intervention planning that can be applied, I want to look at some of the asset classes that have been singled out by Irish legislation for preferential treatment as far as CAT is concerned.

EXEMPT ASSETS

Certain types of assets have been deemed "tax exempt" from an inheritance/gift tax perspective, including:

- ♦ **Forestry:** Investments in "qualifying" forestry assets are exempt from CAT. For example, leaving your heirs €1m in other assets (if the €1m was over and above the tax-free threshold) would result in €200,000 CAT, while leaving

€1m worth of qualifying forestry would mean zero tax being paid.

♦ **Heritage property:** Having one's property formally recognised as a heritage property (basically, a property may qualify for such a registration if it is of some historical, architectural, scientific or social importance to the State) and adhering to other "qualifying" rules will mean it is exempt from CAT in the hands of your heirs.

♦ **Art on public display:** Once a qualifying registration with the relevant Revenue section has been successful, these assets will also be exempt from CAT. This may be the principal reason why unique artworks are now commonly displayed in the reception and other public areas of commercial premises throughout Ireland.

♦ **Irish Government loan paper:** If inherited by individuals not domiciled in the Irish State, these assets can be exempt from local CAT.

♦ **Dwelling house exemption:** Once a certain set of qualifying criteria are met, it is possible for particular individuals to inherit (or receive as a gift) a dwelling house, without being liable to CAT.

♦ **Business and/or agricultural asset relief:** Certain assets of either a business or agricultural nature can be "valued" for inheritance/gift tax purposes at just 10% of their true value.

It is beyond the scope of this book to list all of the exemptions that can be enjoyed and all of the qualifying criteria that need to be met to enjoy them. I just hope that this (less than complete) list demonstrates that intervention planning has the potential to reduce significantly (if not remove altogether) the liabilities that may be suffered by your heirs and, in so doing, offers you the incentive to seek proper, impartial advice on the issue.

So far in this chapter, you have seen that the problems surrounding succession planning may be considerably greater than you have envisaged. This can be true even if your estate is "simple" and without what you would perceive as great value. Also, you now know that, if some of your wealth is surplus to your own requirements, then the investments you make with such surpluses can have a major impact on the taxes to be paid as you part with them (either in life as a gift or in death as an inheritance). Now, I want to outline some of the direct interventions that can be made with the objective of reducing or eliminating future liabilities. I will outline first what I consider to be the principal problem facing anyone attempting a succession plan and then some of the financial structures that can be used.

TAX: THE PRINCIPAL PROBLEM

Notwithstanding the fact that some major problems have already been outlined, and without belittling them in any way, the greatest problem faced by those attempting to plan succession is the ever-changing tax liability.

This is a problem caused by the fact that the tax-free thresholds (TFTs) between donor and beneficiary grow each year in line with inflation, while, if one is enjoying real returns, one's assets are growing at a pace above inflation. If you are not making a real return (a return above inflation) then you are, in fact, losing money and the tax liabilities will fall. However, most people are adding to their cumulative wealth (albeit, in some cases, by accident rather than design) and so, the longer they live, and the wealthier they become, more and more of their accumulated assets will disappear in taxation.

The following graph illustrates this point perfectly:

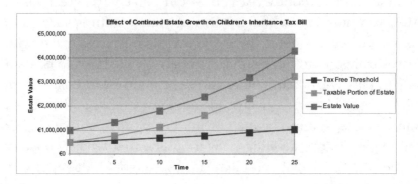

Once financial freedom has been secured for this generation, the graph clearly suggests that accumulating more wealth in the current generation's name(s) may be fundamentally flawed. If assets are surplus to this generation's requirements, then it is "guaranteed" that they will be inherited by your heirs. Accumulating such assets in your name simply further guarantees that 20% of them will be "inherited" by the State rather than by your family. One of the methods that can be used to "turn the tables" in your favour is a trust fund for your children.

TRUST FUNDS FOR CHILDREN

Let us imagine for a moment that you have identified that €993,648 of your existing assets are actually surplus to your needs. You have two young children and have decided to establish a trust fund for each, splitting this surplus cash between the two.

The benefits of such planning are:

♦ Due to the fact that the current (2008) TFT between parent and child is €521,208, the children receive this gift without any immediate tax liability.

♦ Establishing yourself and your spouse as trustees of the new trust funds means that you both continue to control the money and all investment, borrowing, spending or saving decisions are yours to make. Thus, from a control perspective, nothing has changed.

♦ All of the future growth on the money vests in the new owners (the children) and no longer in you. No matter what the value of the trust funds when you finally give the children access, not a single penny in CAT will be payable. This is not to say there will be no tax, but there will be no inheritance or gift tax. Obviously, if the children decide to cash in the investments, it is likely that they will be liable to capital gains tax (CGT) at the same 20% rate as CAT. However, the two major differences to this scenario, when compared to continuing to own the assets yourself and exposing them to CAT when you die, are:

◊ Unlike CAT, which will become automatically payable at some unknown date in the future (the day you die), CGT is a tax one decides to pay. Thus, the fact that it is payable and can be accurately calculated in advance can be taken into the decision-making process.

◊ The CGT payable can be reflected in the asking price your heirs seek as they dispose of the asset(s) in question. The lack of urgency in this sale (when compared to the price one might receive if cash was needed quickly and heavy interest penalties were to be suffered in a CAT situation, as shown earlier) means that these assets will not suffer the erosion of value and your heirs will have the time to demand full and fair value for the assets you worked so hard to create.

- This type of planning procedure also has the potential to deliver multiple TFTs. At this moment in time, when calculating the CAT liabilities of any beneficiary, the Revenue will base its calculation on all gifts and inheritances received since 5 December, 1991. Known as the "aggregation date", when first introduced, it was 1983, it then moved to 1988, and is now 1991. In the event that you live long enough, it is possible that the aggregation date may be moved beyond the date you established the trust funds and thus these gifts may fall outside the CAT net altogether. If you live a very long time, who is to say that it is not possible that you and your family could not enjoy two, three or even four bites of the TFT "cherry"?

- Further gifts, over and above the original TFT, may be transferred to the trust fund without a CAT liability. There will be two opportunities to do this:

  ◊ The first is where you use the annual small gift allowance. A parent is entitled to gift each child up to €3,000 *p.a.*, without incurring a CAT liability. Assuming two living parents, this would allow you to transfer €6,000 to each trust, each year.

  ◊ Secondly, each year, the Budget increases the TFT in line with inflation (for example, in January 2008, the TFT between parent and child increased from €496,824to the current allowance of €521,208). You could choose each year to transfer the increased amount to the trust funds and these transfers will not be subject to CAT.

Time for an example: assume that, having secured your own financial freedom, you find yourself with €1 million of "surplus" cash and decide now to transfer that to your three children via a trust fund today. As each receives €333,333.33, which is below the TFT, no CAT is payable.

Also, now that the money officially belongs to the children, so too does its future value. However, if you had continued to hold the cash in your name, assuming it rises in value by 3% *p.a.* above inflation (at 3% *p.a.* faster than the TFTs), the CAT payable by your children on this portion of your estate will depend on when they inherit. The following table estimates the CAT payable on the value increases at different times in the future:

Term in Years	CAT Payable
5	€31,855
10	€68,783
15	€111,594
20	€161,222

Note: All figures rounded up or down to nearest €1.

So the cash-flow benefits of this type of planning grow as time passes and the underlying value of the assets increase. From a cost point of view, as long as this planning exercise does not cost too much, you and your estate are benefiting hugely. For example, imagine this planning cost you €20,000 to achieve (I am not predicting costs here, as such a planning exercise necessarily will be bespoke and will be priced to reflect your own circumstances), the savings being made (the CAT that would not be payable as indicated by the figures above) over the years represent the following annual internal rates of return (IRR) on the "investment" of €20,000:

Term in Years	IRR
5	9.76%
10	13.15%
15	12.14%
20	11.00%

You can quite clearly see, I hope, how this type of planning reverses the "ever-increasing liability" trend. Earlier, you saw that continuing to hold (surplus) assets in your own name means the longer you live and the wealthier you become, a greater proportion of your estate is exposed to CAT. Now, the longer you live, certainly true for those assets housed within the trust, less and less of your assets are exposed to the tax.

For one reason or another, this planning method may not be effectively applied to certain existing assets. For example, property may not be an ideal candidate for transfer to a child's trust, as such a transfer could immediately expose you (the person doing the transferring) to two costs. First, the ownership transfer will be considered a "disposal" by the donor and this could expose you to CGT. Second, as the property moves from your ownership to that of the trust fund, stamp duty would be payable.

I am not saying that it will never be advantageous to transfer property in this manner, but what I am saying is let mathematics be your guide. If the costs of transfer can be recouped by the future tax savings (the benefits), then a relatively simple mathematical exercise will demonstrate the superior benefits (or not) and this will mean your decision is easier to make.

Other planning interventions can be made where immediate costs would make this one non-profitable. Some of these planning opportunities are briefly described below.

SUBSTITUTION OF ASSETS

If you have (or find yourself in the future with) assets that are surplus to this generation's financial needs, then consideration should be given to "investing" the surpluses in tax-exempt assets (see earlier examples). While an investment in such assets may not be the most exciting you can access, and may not produce the greatest return (although some such assets can enjoy substantial returns), you have to bear in mind the reason for the investment. You are no longer "investing" for yourself (hence the use of inverted commas) nor are you "investing" any longer to produce the greatest return; you are now "investing" with the principal objective of eliminating the tax that your heirs will pay when they inherit your estate. Thus, it may even be prudent to liquidate the surplus assets entirely and to re-invest them in exempt assets.

SHARE CAPPING

As its name suggests, this is an exercise that can cap the value of shares in a private limited company so that their rise in value no longer contributes to the ever-widening gap between the TFTs and your overall net wealth. It works by re-constituting the existing shares in your company, effectively splitting those shares into three separate types of shares. Simply named "A", "B" and "C" shares, each new category can be broadly defined as follows:

- ◆ **"A" shares:** These are generally the current shares as owned by you, renamed. They will never be worth more than the value they hold on the date that share capping is completed.

- ◆ **"B" shares:** These are issued to those to whom you intend to leave the business. They will accumulate all future value increases in the business, which means that, on the day you give them to your heirs, they have little or no real value.

- ◆ **"C" shares:** These are the voting shares in the business and will be retained by the donor (you) for as long as he/she wishes to maintain management control. In the future, these shares may become very useful as, for example, you can give all of your heirs equal value in the business (through the "B" shares and, ultimately, by leaving them the "A" shares after your death), but you can give management control to the one heir who demonstrates the most enthusiasm and/or talent. Often, while we want to treat each of our children fairly and equitably, one or other can show greater business acumen or knowledge of your business and, sometimes, they can pick themselves as your replacement.

Share capping is a complex and expensive exercise to engage in; however, once again pure mathematics will be your guide as to whether the costs are justified by the benefits.

DWELLING HOUSE EXEMPTION

Based on a number of qualifying criteria, which must be met by the beneficiary rather than the person giving the property away, it is possible for you to remove your home (which, in Ireland, is often the single most valuable asset we have to leave) from CAT.

To qualify, in broad terms, the beneficiary must have lived in the house for the previous three years, must not have a financial interest in any other dwelling property and must keep the property for six years after they take ownership (there can be exceptions to this final qualifying criteria – for example, relief may not be clawed back if the property is sold to fund long-term residential medical care). While many of our children may now easily qualify under such criteria, as they get older and move into adulthood, the likelihood of their qualification diminishes. The planning opportunity that may be considered is transferring the home sooner rather than later, when qualification for the exemption is assured.

You have already seen that a transfer of ownership does not necessarily mean a transfer of control. In this case, control may be maintained by using the children's trusts outlined earlier or by simply granting yourself and your spouse a "lifetime interest" in the property as you make the transfer. Therefore, such a change in ownership can be achieved without the current owners losing the decision-making power. Always assuming you are happy that the home will remain in your effective ownership for the rest of your life (future plans to sell and downsize may be a little more difficult to achieve, although not impossible, if ownership is transferred), the benefits of this action can be that you immediately remove a very valuable asset from the inheritance/gift tax net, with potentially huge savings being guaranteed for your heirs. Stamp duty costs (which are half the normal rate, if property is being transferred to your child) will also have to be taken into your cost calculations, as this is a tax that does not arise when assets are transferred on death.

CO-OWNERSHIP (SHAREHOLDER) AGREEMENTS

Such agreements are generally used by partners who own business assets together and/or co-directors of private businesses, to regulate how they interact with each other. Where you hold a minority stake in such a business, I would also recommend that the agreement includes a clause on how shareholdings are valued.

In the event of your death, and in the absence of a formal, legally-binding, agreement, the value of your minority stake is dependent upon the goodwill of your surviving co-owners. Re-writing any current agreement or, in many cases, writing a formal agreement for the first time, should include a valuation clause. This will copper-fasten the value of your stake-holding for your heirs (and, for yourself, if you make it to retirement), a substantial benefit in and of itself. Once the agreement is in place, a further benefit will be provided by insuring each stakeholder for the current value of his/her stake. With "belt and braces" in place, not only have you copper-fastened the value of your assets, but you have also guaranteed that your family will immediately receive full and fair value for that asset should you die prematurely.

There are advantages in this planning procedure for majority stakeholders too. Some in such a position may not have heirs to step into their shoes within the business and they, too, will be interested in turning a stake-holding into cash if they die unexpectedly. Others, who do have an heir waiting in the wings, will want to ensure that the death of a key individual/partner does not bring new, unproductive, stakeholders into the business (*via* the minority stake-holder's family), who perhaps have neither the education nor experience to replace the deceased.

CONCLUSION

In truth, I think I could probably write a whole book on the subject of succession planning – but this is not it. Nonetheless, I hope this chapter demonstrates to you that inheritance tax is not necessarily inevitable (no matter what the value of one's estate) and that well-planned intervention can save huge amounts of money, as well as ensuring your exact wishes are carried out.

Finally, always remember that a lack of planning in this area can lead to posthumous fighting amongst your heirs and such rows (which have a habit of turning legal very quickly) can actually erode your assets to a much greater degree than tax. The newspapers regularly carry stories of families at war over the estates of deceased relatives and seem to revel in reporting the giant legal fees that such fights can incur. A recent story, which revolved around a family pub situated in Dublin city, reported that an estate with an original value of €7.5 million was whittled down to just €3 million after the feuding heirs settled their legal fees.

Neither would I advise that you ignore the potential fighting that could take place after your death with a view like *"My children love each other and would never fight over money"*. While this may well be true, in my experience, it is not the siblings who cause the problems, it is more usually the people your children have married. These people are not as emotionally attached to either the deceased (you) or to their spouse's brothers and sisters (your other children) and so have more appetite for a fight. Neither are they likely to have as much respect for your wishes as your children may have. In short, the most important reason of all to have a properly-structured succession plan may be to save your children the emotional and physical stresses and strains that an unplanned estate could cause them.

9

INVEST TO CREATE INCOME

Once you reach a point in your life where financial freedom is assured, your investment focus will turn from one aimed at creating wealth to one aimed at maintaining that wealth while, at the same time, creating guaranteed income. Many people believe – wrongly, in my opinion – that the two "masters" of growth and income can be served within the one investment strategy. Indeed, it is no wonder that many believe this as the investment product manufacturers will happily sell you products to do both. But, the fact that a particular investment product can pay you an income does not automatically mean you should use it to do so.

Most investment products that provide an "income facility" fall under the broad description of unit-linked funds. The type of investments one can get exposure to within these funds typically fit into the following categories:

- Stocks and shares.
- Property.
- Government loan stock (gilts).
- Cash.

While there are many, many different funds available, the reality is that a huge percentage of such funds have an investment allocation across all of these categories and carry the name "managed funds". While I do not intend to re-visit the various problems from which this type of fund suffers (internal costs and a one-size-fits-all investment strategy being just two; you may wish to re-read **Chapter 2** if you have forgotten the others), I do want to explain why I believe this is a misnomer. The name "managed fund" conjures up images of active management, where a fund manager, or perhaps even a group of fund managers, are changing the funds' exposure to the different asset classes as and when they feel the time is right to be more or less exposed to one over and above another. Indeed, much of the marketing literature produced around these funds, at least, hints at such a practice and the salesman is likely to confirm it as one of the reasons why you should invest. Certainly, when I was involved in the sale of such products, I was taught to say to people things like *"Why make the investment decisions yourself when a team of professionals can make them for you?"*. If you are already an investor in managed funds, perhaps that sales pitch sounds familiar?

The reason managed fund, in my view, is the wrong title is that, in truth, there is very little "management" at all. In my experience, such funds rarely alter their allocation to the various assets, with any major shift in allocation being caused by inflows and outflows of cash, rather than being influenced by any alteration in the manager's view. Thus, they should in my opinion be called "mixed funds" rather than "managed funds". In my view, investing in such a fund with the expectation of active, professional, management of your money, to your specific risk profile and term to liquidity, is a recipe for disappointment.

The term unit-linked fund comes from the fact that such funds are divided into units, the value of which rises and falls with the performance of the underlying investment. For example, a fund valued at, say, €100m in total, with 1,000,000 units issued in that fund, will have a unit price of €100. If you have €100,000 invested, then you have been allocated 1,000 units in the fund. If you are receiving an "income" from such a fund, it is most likely that, at the start, you chose a percentage income rate, say 4% for this example. This percentage applies to the amount of investment and thus an annual income of €4,000 can be expected.

It is the manner used to deliver your income that is the problem. As and when the income falls due for payment, the investment product provider will simply "sell" enough units in the fund so that the income can be paid. Sticking with our example, and assuming the €4,000 *p.a.* is to be paid monthly at a unit price of €100, then to pay your €333.33 monthly amount, the investment company will cash in 3.33 units in your fund. However, as unit prices can fall as well as rise, let us imagine your fund had suffered a 10% loss on the day prior to your income being paid. The unit price, when your income comes to be paid, has fallen to €90 and to pay your €333.33 requires the encashment of 3.7 units – effectively, 10% more of your units must be cashed to provide your monthly income payment. And here lies the problem. Most managed funds have *circa* 70% of their investments allocated to the stock market and while, over any reasonable length of time, you can expect decent returns from that market (the amount of which you will actually receive being completely dependent upon the charges within the fund), those returns will be achieved in a volatile way. Some days, markets will rise, on others, they will fall, and the timing of those ups and downs will play a major role in the value for money you are receiving.

Again, let us use an example to illustrate my point. In the paragraph above, you saw that a 10% drop in the unit price, which unfortunately occurred the day before your income became payable, cost you an extra 10% of your units. However, let us imagine that, the day after you took your income, the markets bounced back with a 25% rise (the €90 unit price rose to €103.50 the day after you "sold"). The 3.7 units you "sold" yesterday for €333.33 would be worth €382.95 and the poor timing of the sale actually cost you considerably more than the earlier figure suggests.

Automatic income from such funds is exactly that – automatic. No one is paying attention to the value you are actually getting and a series of "bad timings" where your income is concerned can rapidly erode your cash, even in a fund that year-to-year actually posts a positive investment return.

One figure I have not included here is tax which, on many withdrawals from such funds, can be levied at 23% on your "profit" element (some of the income you get will be deemed a return of your original investment amount and non-taxable) and I have done so deliberately. Tax, dependent upon when you set up your unit-linked fund, may be as described or may actually be within the fund itself; each method has a slightly different effect on the income. Also, tax does nothing to further my message, as the ineffectiveness of such products in producing "income" is not affected, one way or the other, by tax.

There is one more major reason why such funds should not be used for income creation – there is a better way. In our business, when we approach income planning for those clients we have brought to financial freedom, we set the following objectives:

♦ To produce the required income in as guaranteed an environment as possible.

♦ To achieve the above in as tax efficient a manner as possible.

The first objective recognises that, once your financial freedom has been secured, the need to take on investment risk has substantially diminished. It is also my experience that the older we get, the more financially conservative we tend to become (probably due to the fact that we have, arguably, less time to recoup) and so our first objective tends to suit clients who have achieved their financial targets. The second objective should, by now, not surprise any reader as you are well aware that creating income and keeping income are two completely different things.

In such circumstances, my preference is to use a relatively standard, fixed term, deposit account to produce the income. As I see it, the two main benefits of this vehicle, when attempting to create a guaranteed income stream, are:

♦ Over the fixed term (say six years) a guaranteed interest rate can be secured and thus, once the mathematics are correct, the investor can be sure of receiving a guaranteed level of income for a guaranteed period, with risk kept to an absolute minimum.

♦ By using a deposit fund, any taxation to be paid is limited to the deposit interest retention tax (DIRT) rate of just 20% (PRSI and/or levies may be applied to this of income, but their application depends on the personal circumstances of the individual involved).

The best way to illustrate what I mean is to give you an example. Let's imagine an investor has €1.5 million in cash and has decided to take it easy and stop working. He/she has told me that they require an income of €50,000 *p.a.* after tax and has asked me to make a recommendation.

Following the two main objectives above, I will first search the market for the best deposit rate over the next six years from a deposit taker that has the facility to pay out an automatic income to a normal bank account. I am aware that a slightly better rate may be available, for example, from the online banks but I am also aware that dealing with these providers can mean considerable work on the part of the investor. They tend to provide simple deposit accounts with no income-paying facilities, so this would mean the investor having to deal proactively with the online bank's website to receive the income (which could be on 12 separate occasions each year, if he/she wanted monthly payments). Some will consider this too much hassle for the slightly increased rate, while others will recognise that an illness, a power-cut at home and many more incidents outside of your control could interfere with your income being paid on time.

So, having researched the market, I have been told that a rate of 3.75% *p.a.* can be guaranteed over the next six years. The deposit provider will also pay the required income automatically to a current account on a monthly basis. Now the question is how much cash will have to be placed on deposit to guarantee €50,000 *p.a.*, net of taxes? The amount required will be: €274,922.50.

As the investor draws the €50,000 p.a. income (€300,000 over the six years), the bulk of this will be deemed a "return of capital" and will be completely tax-free. Over the six-year term, the account will draw down to zero. So, for a deposit of €274,922.50, the investor will receive €300,000 in total net income and will have paid total tax (DIRT) of: €6,269.38. This is a tax liability of just €87.07 per month.

The beauty of this planning procedure is that the remaining cash of €1,225,077.50 (the original €1.5m less the €274,922.50 that will be deposited to provide income over the next six years) can now be invested exclusively for growth. There will be no need for income to be produced over the six-year period and, using your new-found knowledge, you can choose a tax-free roll-up fund to house the remaining capital. In this way, over the initial six-year period, the €6,269.38 DIRT that is paid will be the only tax payable. For the growth fund to replace the €274,922.50 that you have spent, the growth will need to be 3.43% *p.a.* before exit tax, or 4.46% *p.a.* after tax (which you may decide not to pay in full, as the total growth fund would not have to be encashed totally – bearing in mind the "8-year rule" discussed earlier, which means that every eight years the profit from such products is now taxed, whether you draw out that profit or not).

Your growth fund will be best positioned to achieve the growth required to maintain your capital value as it pays no internal tax. If that money was invested outside of such a fund, and liable to the top tax and levy deductions of 46%, for example, the gross growth you would have to achieve rises to 6.35% *p.a.* Thus, outside of the tax-free roll-up structure, more risk (the greater the risk, the greater the potential for losses or gains) needs to be taken to maintain the value of your capital.

I do not present this structure as the one most likely to give you the best possible return but it is one of the best ways I know of limiting the risk to ongoing income and of minimising taxation. In six years' time, the structure will have to be re-negotiated and the figures then will depend upon where deposit rates have gone and how well (or badly) your growth fund has grown.

The principal point I wanted to make in this chapter is that investing to create wealth is a very different endeavour from investing to produce income and/or to maintain wealth. While it could be argued here that I am being over-cautious with my suggestions, the true nature of the risk associated with them cannot be gauged unless and until the investment allocation of the tax-free roll-up fund is decided upon. Such funds are available from an abundance of product providers (insurance companies and banks being the major providers in the Irish marketplace) and with investment allocations to suit all risk preferences. Not only are the broad asset classes available in particular funds labelled property, equities, cash and gilts (which, if described this way, are likely to have a broad allocation across a number of different markets), but more focused investment can be provided under funds labelled, for example, Japanese equity, German property, emerging markets, etc. You will need to pay close attention to the terms and conditions of the funds themselves, to satisfy yourself that value for money and expertise are being provided (which now you can do, using the information contained in **Chapter 2**).

Once you have satisfied yourself on these issues, such funds will allow you take as much or as little risk as you desire. You have already seen that, in the figures illustrated earlier, to match the real investment performance of these funds while making investments in your own name (such as, for example, purchasing stocks and shares direct), you would need to outperform the tax-free roll-up fund by *circa* 42% (the return you would need to produce within personally held assets is 42% higher than the return required inside a tax-free roll-up fund).

It is also worth mentioning that I have approached this chapter on the assumption that, in the recommendation given earlier, the €1.5m is the totality of this person's assets. This is the money that, if managed properly, will provide our imaginary investor with financial freedom for the rest of his imaginary life. If this was not the case (but if €1.5m was all that was required to guarantee his/her financial future), then my recommendations would alter dramatically.

I might make recommendations around some of the ideas outlined in **Chapter 8**, transferring some, if not all, of the surplus assets to the next generation. If there was no next generation, other options would be considered, from more aggressive investments (although, where possible, I would still house these within a tax-free roll-up fund) to the creation of a charitable trust.

Finally, assuming additional assets are maintained by the imaginary client (which, for one reason or another, cannot be transferred to the next generation immediately), the investment make-up of these assets will affect the recommendation to be made for his/her income-producing assets. The reason why other assets should affect a decision is risk: if you do not take such additional assets into account (or, worse still, if your adviser is unaware of them), then you could end up increasing your exposure to one type of asset (such as shares or property) and, in so doing, increasing risk without necessarily recognising the increase.

10
UNDERSTANDING RISK & REWARD

Continuing with the theme running through this book, often it is the way we perceive risk that diminishes our ability to create true financial freedom. In my experience, most people perceive risk in a very black-and-white manner, which leads to statements such as: *"I would never invest in something where I could lose all."*

The problem, in my view, with a personal mantra such as this one is that it immediately removes, from the particular investor who utters it, the ability to invest in some of the world's greatest wealth-creation assets. I would agree with the statement if it was slightly altered to the following: *"I would never invest **all of my money** in something where I could lose all."*

Although a subtle difference, it is this difference that could have a huge impact on your ability to create wealth. Without fear of too much contradiction, one can state that, no matter what the potential reward, risking it all (potentially turning yourself into a homeless vagrant) is too great a risk to take. However, for example, risking 5% of your wealth with the potential of increasing that wealth by, say, 50% is a very different proposition indeed. The person who lives by the first mantra above would refuse even to consider such an investment, while those living with the second mantra will consider it on what is known as a risk/reward basis.

Indeed, this is the main point I want to make about risk. One can only judge the true nature of it, once the potential reward is taken into account. Let me illustrate my point with an example already highlighted in **Chapter 2**. One of the most expensive charges within manufactured investment products is the annual management fee. You have seen that this charge can be relatively high or low and, in and of itself, has the potential to seriously affect your real returns. I stated that it is not a matter of simply trawling the market for the lowest fee possible (in what arena is cheapest automatically considered the best?), but of ensuring that you convince yourself that an increased fee is likely to deliver an increased benefit. Earlier, I did not describe this decision as a risk/reward decision, but that is what it is.

It is also important for anyone who harbours an ambition to create true financial freedom to recognise that such an ambition is, in my opinion, incompatible with risk-free investment. The first thing to tell you is that, in reality, "risk-free investment" is non-existent and, yes, while there are investments that will guarantee a fixed return (for example, deposit accounts), these are not "risk-free".

The reason that no investment can be described as "risk-free" is inflation. Every year, the purchasing power of our money is decreased by inflation and, over time, even a modest inflation rate has the ability to erode real value substantially. To illustrate my point, the following table gives you the today's value equivalent of €10,000 over various timeframes, assuming an average inflation rate of 3% *p.a.* (which is *circa* 2% less than the Irish inflation rate for 2006, and thus could be considered a conservative figure).

Term	Today's Value Equivalent of €10,000 @ 3% *p.a.* inflation
5 years	€8,626
10 years	€7,440
15 years	€6,418
20 years	€5,537
25 years	€4,776

So, to put it another way, if today your €10,000 would buy you 10,000 apples, after 25 years of 3% *p.a.* inflation, your €10,000 will only buy you 4,776 apples.

For some people, the realisation that every investment you can make has an element of risk opens the way to a complete re-evaluation of their attitudes towards risk. For others, further challenges to their current beliefs may be necessary and, in my experience, at least some simply refuse to even entertain the idea of reviewing those beliefs. One of the ways some of these people comfort themselves in their "risk-free" (and now you know there is no such thing) world is they describe themselves as "conservative". This is the way, for example, my father would describe himself now (he's 76), but it is also how he would have described himself throughout his life.

During a recent conversation with him the topic of risk arose and, once more, the "conservative" handle was used.

"Sorry, Dad", I replied, *"but I don't buy that description anymore. The truth of the matter is that people who describe themselves as 'conservative' would actually describe themselves as 'afraid' if they were being brutally honest."*

My father thought about this for a moment, started to say something and then stopped, thought some more and then said: *"I suppose that's true, if I was brutally honest with myself"*.

Of course, I did not say this to my father to embarrass or ridicule him in any way, and if you describe yourself as "conservative" and I made these comments to you, the same would be true. I say it because I believe that, at times, some of us hide behind such descriptions. It is far more comfortable to describe oneself as "conservative" than it is to admit (even if just to oneself) to being "afraid".

I dealt with the topic of financial fear earlier and I do not intend to dwell on it too much here. But fear almost always is rooted in a lack of knowledge, experience or skill (for example, the fear of open water is usually overcome by learning to swim).

In my view, learning to judge risk is of paramount importance as without such knowledge and skill, as an investor, you will either:

♦ Fail to make the investments necessary to produce real returns (over and above the inflation rate) and will see, over time, the true value of your investments fall.

♦ Have the wool pulled over your eyes by well-constructed "sales pitches" and find yourself invested in assets that are not what you perceived them to be.

To judge risk effectively, you need to have the answers, in writing, to the following questions:

♦ **Maximum potential returns:** What are the maximum returns that could be provided and what evidence can be shown that proves the potential? Past performance (remember, you want to see an historical investment, the amount invested, the amount the investor received back, less any tax payable, and an indication of the annual return represented by these figures) will be a good guide. If the past is being used to justify your decision to invest, ask why the seller believes the past circumstances will be repeated. Also, ask what circumstances would have to exist for a poor performance to be delivered and why, in the seller's opinion, such circumstances are unlikely.

◆ **Maximum potential losses:** By knowing exactly the potential loss that could be suffered, you are in a far better position to decide how much, if any, of your money you might invest. Once again, in and of itself, this information is practically useless but, when compared with the maximum potential return, you can judge value. Being asked to risk 100% of your investment for a potential return of 5% *p.a.*, for example, is unlikely to attract your attention; however, the same 100% risk with a potential of a 700% return may be enough for you to risk some of your wealth.

◆ **Term of the investment and the exit mechanism:** If, for example, you were going to invest directly in a property, the term is likely to be up to you, but you can still ask the seller for his best guess at capital appreciation for the next few years. Exiting such an investment obviously requires you to sell the property. However, if you are considering an off-the-shelf investment, then ensure that the proposed term of the investment suits your timeframe and that a well-structured, definitive, exit mechanism is in place. Often, such investments can be vague about the exit. Future exit may require a majority decision from the investors and who is to say that the time-scales of the majority will fit with your own? Worse still, in my opinion, is an exit that is controlled by the sellers (who are often in receipt of an ongoing fee), their interests may not be aligned with those of the investors. You need to ask as many questions as are necessary to ensure you fully understand their terms and conditions.

◆ **Tax payable:** The taxes to be paid, either directly by the investor or internally within the product, will impact on the success or otherwise of the investment. Indeed, I have seen investment products that, based on the marketing literature, appear to provide a reasonable risk/reward ratio but, when taxes are applied, look decidedly less attractive. From now on, you need only be interested in net (after tax) reward, as you are now only interested in the wealth you get to keep. Finally, if you are the owner of a private pension fund, it will always be worth asking whether a particular investment can be housed within such a vehicle. If the answer is "Yes", then Irish income tax and capital gains tax generally is not levied, as long as the Revenue rules are followed.

Receiving answers, in writing (don't forget the Financial Regulator's mantra: "if it isn't in writing, it doesn't exist") to these questions (along with those outlined in **Chapter 2**, when dealing with manufactured product) will provide you with far greater knowledge than ever before. May I predict that, when you start to judge risk in this manner, your own attitude to risk will change?

Despite what anyone thinks or believes, risk is not a black-and-white issue; it is more shades of grey. Also, despite what anyone thinks or believes, you will have a far greater chance of achieving true financial freedom if you are prepared to take some risk. It is the lack of ability to judge – or even recognise – risk that is the greatest challenge facing the individual investor. The inability to recognise risk is one that, when the true risk is pointed out, most people are truly surprised by.

In my day job, every new client is put through a process we call risk-profiling. Using seven separate risk statements, we ask all full-service clients to tell us which of the statements most closely describes the risk they are willing to take. Once a choice has been made, we then apply a risk rating to that client (a numerical scale of 1 to 7) and review all of their existing financial arrangements (this is something we do as we take on the client) with their risk rating in mind. Invariably, we find that those who choose one of the low risk statements have actually taken on more risk in their past than they perceived. Funnily enough, the opposite is generally true of those who choose the higher risk statements, who have typically taken on less risk.

If the majority of readers of this book are similar in make-up to the clients of my business, then the inability to judge risk (and/or the inability to describe the type of risk they may be prepared to take) is endemic amongst the population in general. This should not surprise anyone, as it simply shows that, as well as never being taught about money itself (how to earn it, how to invest it, how to borrow and repay it…), we are never taught about investment risk either. In the past, I have seen people who describe themselves as "conservative" take on very high risk investments, not because their attitude to risk has altered in any way but simply because they do not recognise the risk in the first place. This type of risk mis-management is rife where tax-based property is concerned. Investors who do not apply a "risk identification process" (asking all the questions outlined here and in **Chapter 2** and demanding the answers in writing) are often distracted by some special feature of the item for sale. Tax-breaks are, admittedly, quite a distraction but every investment needs to be properly investigated as an investment first; tax-breaks, may I suggest, should be viewed as the icing on the cake.

Distractions that I have witnessed include:

- ◆ **Personal preference:** A particular problem for investors in residential property, where the fact that you would like to live in it yourself (and not buying somewhere you would not live in yourself) is one of the major reasons for the purchase. Whether or not you would reside in it is of little or no importance to the investment decision (unless, of course, that is the intention). Purchasing a property in this manner rarely has any financial merit as:

◊ Neither you, nor people like you (if they are like you, they are unlikely to be renting residential property, they will have their own house), are going to reside in it.

◊ Greater value, greater yields and greater capital appreciation are more likely to be enjoyed in other, more up-and-coming, areas.

♦ **Friendship:** I mentioned at the very start of this book that emotions are less than useful when it comes to financial decision-making. While I made this comment about fear and greed, I wish to extend it here to personal loyalty. Every day, people invest in things that are promoted or sold by their friends, justifying their decision with *"He's a friend of mine and I'd like to help him out"*, or a variation on that theme. There is nothing worse than when an investment, delivered to you by a friend (or family member perhaps), goes wrong. The very friendship that drove you to make the investment in the first place turns the financial loss into a personal problem and the friendship that you tried to cement with the investment can fall apart. The "helping out" rationale for making the investment, which did provide some financial assistance to the seller when you purchased, is now the rock on which the friendship perishes. If a personal friend of mine wishes to deal with my business, then I make two things abundantly clear from the start: first, they will not be dealing with me; second, they must recognise that, in the event of a result less than expected (the risk being fully explained and accepted beforehand), I cannot, and **will not**, interfere.

♦ **Someone else did it:** I cannot count the number of times that this has been the answer to *"Why did you make this particular investment?"*. The fact that a friend, a neighbour, the captain of the local golf club, your accountant, etc, made an investment is no reason whatsoever for you to follow suit. It is certainly no reason to abandon a proper risk evaluation process. The "someone else" probably has a different attitude to risk than you have, may have a different investment horizon in sight, simply may not have been able to judge the risk for themselves. Thus, you could be investing in something that has more or less risk than suits you, which will mature too early or too late for your plans, or you may simply be repeating the mistakes of "someone else".

♦ **I needed the tax-break:** As you saw with the Section 23 property example earlier (see **Chapter 3**), I make the assumption that you will pay above normal market value for any investment offering tax concessions (that is why, earlier, I did not assume the Section 23 property would rise in value). In many historical tax-based investments, the painful truth is that the investor would have been better off paying the tax and investing the net amount, even in a deposit account.

♦ **It's what, or all, I know:** Investing, and in many cases over-investing, in a particular type of asset, just because it is what you are familiar with, leads to increased risks that, for many, are not recognised. In Ireland, the typical over-exposure is to property, where private investors have enjoyed substantial benefits over the last two decades. Many have failed to recognise that one only gets larger rewards when taking larger risks.

It is only the investor who does not have a risk identification process who will be distracted by these issues. You now have such a process available to you and, if you apply it, your future investment decisions will take all costs, all benefits and all risks into account which, in turn, will lead to better decisions.

Finally, where risk is concerned, never lose sight of the fact that a diversity of different assets reduces risk. The two major investment assets (of equities and property) often are growing in opposite directions, depending upon the prevailing economic environment and an investment "foot in both camps" can serve to reduce overall risk substantially.

And never forget that even once you have made your investment decision, you still have one final decision to make – *how* you will invest! With your new knowledge, future investments will be made within private pension funds or perhaps tax-free roll-up funds. Borrowing will be introduced, even where it is not needed, to accelerate your rate of real wealth creation. You may even decide to make certain investments in the name of other family members, using bespoke structures (for example, children's trusts) both to retain control and to limit the effects of future taxation.

I mentioned at the beginning of this chapter that risk tends to be viewed in a very black-and-white manner; most people allow fear to stand in the way of a better and brighter financial future. Much of this fear will be erased as your knowledge improves and as you become familiar with actually taking risk. But, let me warn you: the fear never goes away altogether – it is always there in the background. This is not a bad thing, in my view, as it is the fear itself that will ensure you pay attention to detail and ask all the right questions.

Much of my professional life is now spent on my feet in front of audiences and some will tell you that public speaking is extremely frightening. I remember well the first time I spoke in public: quite literally, I threw up in a bucket seconds before taking to the podium! The fear I experienced then was so great that it caused a physical reaction. However, I got through it, practised, got some help and training from those more experienced than I was and now I do about 20 to 30 speaking engagements a year. Every time, just before I go on, I feel the fear bubbling in the pit of my stomach. No longer strong enough to cause me to part with my breakfast, but it is still there, ever-present, only now I have control over it.

As you become an investor (or expand your investments), you too are going to have a similar experience. The question is: how will you deal with it? Perhaps the following will help. Concentrating on the two most popular investment assets of property and equities, try to answer this question:

> *"What would have to happen for an investment in such assets, over time, to actually lose me money?"*

My answers are:

- ◆ **Property:** While I can convince myself that a property I buy today could be less valuable over a short period of time (caused, for example, by a sharp rise in interest rates), I cannot convince myself that over a long period the same will happen. Over the longer-term, it is bound to rise in value, with inflation, if nothing else. The wood in the windows, the tiles on the floor, the fixtures and fittings and the labour required to put them all together will rise with inflation and so too will the value of your investment property. To convince yourself otherwise, you will have to convince yourself of some catastrophic world event ruining the economy of the Western world. If this happens, the last thing we will be worried about is the value of our property. Survival, plain and simple, is most likely to be the main priority.

- ◆ **Equities:** Again, over a relatively short period of time, I can convince myself that world markets (I am referring to index-tracker-style investments here, buying just one share is much more risky) will fall. I am also well aware of what global events can do to the world's markets (as the two

Gulf wars have demonstrated). However, to decide to
avoid these investments over the longer-term, I would
have to convince myself that the world's greatest
companies will never grow their profits again.
Furthermore, I would have to convince myself that all
mergers and acquisitions activity will cease and that there
will never again be another new invention that everyone
wants to buy. I do not know about you, but I cannot
convince myself of these points (other than in the same
catastrophic environment described earlier).

Creating sustainable financial freedom is something that takes
time and so, relatively speaking, short-term fluctuations are
irrelevant. Of course, one has to factor-in the potential of such
short-term events into one's pre-investment mathematical
calculations (especially true, if money is to be borrowed to make
an investment). One has to be convinced that such short-term
events could not cause an early, forced exit from the investment,
which could happen, for example, if repayments on a loan were
missed. As before, proper pre-investment planning will be your
guide.

Also, I believe that we must run our financial lives on the
assumption that catastrophe will not strike. After all, if it does
there is little or nothing we will be able to do about it and, as
already stated, the currency of the day will change to food,
shelter and water, money will be useless. However, if
catastrophe is avoided, and yet we have failed to provide for our
future because the fear of a catastrophic event froze us to the
spot, then we will have failed to make provision and yet be still
living in a world where money is vital.

So, creating wealth is about time and not timing. 'Timing' is
the battle-cry of the product-sellers because they want you to
invest now; after all, their job is to get you to buy! Many
examples of how the timing of a particular investment improves
the result can be given. But, just as "one swallow does not a

summer make", neither does one investment make financial freedom. The result of one particular investment has a limited effect on your overall attempts to create real wealth. Real wealth will be achieved more easily, if an integrated and structured plan is put into action. Within this plan, investments are just a small (*albeit* vital) part of the process. Tax planning, wealth creation structures, the re-structuring of your financial past and regular reviews to take account of changing circumstances are just as important.

Risk, in reality, is diluted over time; the longer you have to invest, the more likely a positive outcome.

11
KNOWLEDGE IS (TRULY) KING

You probably have realised by now that one of the objectives in writing this book is to incentivise the reader to increase financial knowledge. During a recent seminar I was giving in Donegal, I used the well-known statement, *"Knowledge is king"* and, to my surprise, I was challenged by an audience member.

"No", he argued, *"knowledge is not king – the application of knowledge is king!"*

I had to agree with my critic; of course, he was right. No matter what new information may have been imparted as you read this work, it is all completely useless to you, if you do not apply it.

Applying the new learning of this book will take time and effort and, if you are like most people, the time will be very hard to find. Our lives are busy and, unless you consistently find yourself with little or nothing to do, this probably means you will have to steal the time from other areas of your life. If I may make a suggestion: the place to steal the time from is your income generation activities. You are now aware that income generation is a very different discipline from wealth creation. In my experience, most working people spend 100% of their work-effort on generating income and nothing at all on creating wealth. While such an apportionment of time will maximise one's income, if the financial results of the vast bulk of workers are anything to go by, real wealth will never be achieved.

We all have to recognise that, for one reason or another, the time will come when we can no longer generate income. Whether this is true because our employer will deem us too old, or we simply tire of the rat-race, or it is forced upon us by physical infirmity, the day will come. Even for those of us lucky enough to have a good business that is to be passed on to the next generation, no guarantee of income can be given (and, as I mentioned earlier, drawing income from a business as it is passed on to less experienced management may not be ideal). So, other than for the super-rich (and, even for them, there are riches-to-rags horror stories), one day, income will cease and the real question is whether we will be ready for this. The standard planning one can do to prepare for this event, such as having a pension, repaying the home loan, becoming debt-free, etc will replace some income but, typically, not all.

Consider the pension allowances for a moment. For the self-employed (sole trader or those in non-pensionable employment), there are fixed caps on how much one can invest tax efficiently and, thus, how much can actually be accumulated *via* this off-the-shelf product. For the proprietary director, a maximum of two-thirds final salary, less any lump sum commuted and paid tax-free as you retire, is allowable. Put yourself in this place for a moment: you have now reached normal retirement age and are given two-thirds the income you had the day before, with 24 hours a day to spend your own money. "Yesterday" your income was 33% more and, on average, for eight hours a day you had little opportunity to spend that income. "Today", your days are no longer filled with business meetings or appointments, there is nowhere to be by 9am five days a week. Now you have to amuse yourself. Certainly, even today, I cannot seem to leave my home for any purpose without coming home €50 "lighter". How will you deal with this? What is it that you enjoy doing today that you will have to stop doing? Can you still afford the golf club fees, the regular foreign holidays, the two cars in the driveway, etc?

Earlier, I stated that we tend to live life *via* "sound-bite" financial advice. One such sound bite that was quoted at me as I prepared to leave full-time education was "get a good, pensionable job" and I followed that advice for around 17 years afterwards. However, 17 years on, I was, in truth, no richer or poorer than when I started and was on the same path as my father had travelled. It was then that I realised that sticking to the same path would lead me to the same destination. I, too, was preparing to "invest" *circa* 40 years of my life for the "reward" of a relatively basic retirement. Just like the character in Shakespeare's *Hamlet*, this sound-bite advice was offered to me by a concerned parent who wanted the best for me, who wanted to protect me and so the rationale behind it could not be questioned. My father had received the same advice from his father and had improved his lifestyle considerably when compared to that enjoyed by his parents, so he passed it on to me.

In doing so, he failed to recognise that the world is a very different place today than it was when he left school (1954). He also failed to recognise that, together, he and my mother had provided me with more opportunities than ever existed when he left school. We were discussing this recently during a family dinner, where both my father and his older brother were commenting on how much better off their children were than themselves.

"Yes", I answered, *"because we are standing on the shoulders of giants. If you guys had not done what you did, had not paid the fees to educate us, had not made the financial sacrifices, had not, in essence, followed the sound-bite financial advice, then much of what your children have achieved may not have been possible."*

Today, in a relatively free world, there are more opportunities to create real wealth than have ever existed throughout human history. Not only this, but by applying true financial intelligence, nearly everyone in the Western world can take advantage of these opportunities. No matter who you are, or what level income you generate, financial freedom is possible. The real question is, do you want it badly enough?

Your "desire" is what will determine whether you actually apply the new knowledge that this book (and my previous one) imparts. Applying the new knowledge will mean change and, for most of us, change is uncomfortable.

I now run a series of financial coaching seminars and, before starting, I ask attendees three simple questions:

- ◆ Do you wish to be financially free?
- ◆ Do you believe that you will become financially free?
- ◆ Have you done anything about achieving financial freedom?

It will not surprise anyone that 100% of attendees answer *"Yes"* to the first question, but only 70% answer *"Yes"* to the second and just 40% answer *"Yes"* to the third.

To the 30% of people who "do not believe", I challenge them to deal with that first. No matter what new techniques I can outline to these people, no matter how much they understand them and recognise the logic behind them, these people will do nothing. One reason they will do nothing is, quite simply, they "do not believe" it will make a difference. None of these people can deny that financial freedom can and does exist, there are far too many financially-free people in the public eye to allow such denial. However, as a friend of mine is inclined to say, *"people get in life what they expect, the truth of which comes from people's beliefs"*. If you believe something possible, then taking the actions to achieve the objective is relatively easy; if you do not believe, taking the necessary actions is, in your mind, "useless".

So, applying the knowledge is king, not the knowledge itself. Also, the more knowledge you can gain, the more financial intelligence you will have at your disposal, and the better your financial decisions will be in the future. Thus, I am suggesting that your drive for new financial intelligence should not end with finishing this book. There are many other ways of improving your knowledge and you should be taking as much advantage of them as you possibly can.

One of the most interesting developments of the recent past has been the emergence of investment courses, which generally concentrate on educating their students on stock market investment. Two courses I have personally experienced are run by The Investment Club Network Ltd. (TICN) and *Invest like the Best Ltd*. Indeed, it was the managing director of TICN who was in the audience when I said "knowledge is king" and who (by questioning this statement and adding the all-important "application of") is indirectly responsible for this chapter. Each of these organisations offer their students new and/or improved knowledge, so that they can be confident about investing in the world's greatest wealth-generating assets.

In addition to improving your own knowledge, for most people, there will be a need to increase opportunity too. If, in the past, you have simply purchased off-the-shelf, generic financial products or received advice from people paid to sell you stuff, then until you change something, this is all that is likely to be presented in the future. In the very first chapter, I suggested how you should go about choosing a financial adviser for the future. If you apply this new knowledge, then your new adviser no doubt will introduce you to new and exciting projects. However as we say in our business, nobody has a monopoly on good ideas and therefore it may be worth your while letting others know of your interests. Within *Financial Engineering Network Ltd.*, on average, 30% to 50% of the investments our clients make they source themselves. Our job is to help them identify all costs, benefits and risks and thus to decide whether a particular investment is value for money and whether it fits with their overall risk profile.

Get yourself a list of all registered investment intermediaries (available from the Financial Regulator[6]) and call each one (OK, at least those within easy geographical reach) to ask what type of investments they are involved with and, if they sound interesting, ask to be placed on their mailing list. Become a prolific reader of specialist magazines and newspapers; often, they have details of investment vehicles that you would not otherwise come across. In short, make true wealth accumulation part of your daily routine. If you do not, may I suggest that when you reach a point in your life when you would like to stop working but cannot, you have no right to be disappointed or surprised. Just as the regular worker who reaches age 65 and is "rewarded" with two-thirds his/her salary (and now has 24 hours a day to spend it) has no right to have expected any other outcome, neither will you. One cannot expect wealth, if one does nothing about achieving wealth!

It would be remiss of me, in completing this chapter, not to state that, if you have neither the time nor the inclination to DIY true wealth accumulation, then consider paying someone else to help you do it. As the joint-owner of a business that specialises in this area, I would be missing a great opportunity for self-promotion if I failed to mention paying a third party. There is no doubt that paying someone else to help will increase the costs,

---

6   In Ireland, the Financial Regulator (PO Box 9138, College Green, Dublin 2 – phone: 01 410 4000 – email: consumerinfo@financialregulator.ie – web: www.financialregulator.ie).

but you now know that, in and of itself, this is unimportant. The benefit of paying someone else is that it actually gets done (rather than it being placed on the long finger and, maybe, never being done at all) and, with a true financial adviser at your side it is likely that the risks will be diminished too. Paying someone else is not something that should scare us or, worse, stop us from taking action. I have said it before, when you want to learn any new skill you generally seek out a professional, pay him/her a fee to teach you new techniques and then practice those new techniques until your "game" improves. This is true, if you want to learn to play better golf, to learn to play tennis, to learn to use computers, and it is also true, if you want to learn to create real financial freedom.

In purchasing this book, you have taken a major step in the right direction. Please do not let this be your last step.

12

... And That's What Gets Results!

To quote the words of the song:

> ♫ *"It ain't what you do, it's the way that you do it ... and that's what gets results"* ♫

When I first chose this tag-line for the front cover, I could not remove the song from my head for many days afterwards. If you suffer similarly, I apologise, but you certainly could live your financial life far less successfully than by this musical mantra.

You now know that it is the **way** you go about your financial affairs that has far greater potential to create real wealth than **where** you choose to invest. You now know that people who carry business cards with titles like "financial adviser" or "financial consultant", etc may not necessarily be what they appear to be. Most such card-carriers in Ireland are actually paid to sell you products and the way you go about choosing your financial adviser (or, perhaps re-interviewing your existing adviser) will impact heavily on your efforts to create wealth.

Furthermore, you have recognised that wealth creation is a very different skill from income generation and that, in order to eventually stop working without having a serious deterioration in lifestyle, requires you to master both skills. Financial institutions, while the products they provide have an integral part to play in your wealth creation efforts, are not there to impart advice and are inherently conflicted (despite the fact that current legislation allows them to call themselves "advisers"). These institutions are, in fact, no different than other high-street retailers. They need your business to survive and prosper. Not so long ago I wrote an article for *The Investor* magazine under the rather long-winded title of:

> *"When will the banks start to act like the consumer businesses that they are?"*

My conclusion was very simple. The banks will act like consumer businesses when we start to treat them as such. We cannot change the financial institutions. For them and their shareholders, nothing needs changing, their profit margins are extremely healthy and their share prices are rising. All we can hope to change is ourselves and, in changing the way we interact with these financial monoliths, to change the result we are getting from our money. Eventually, if enough of us make the change, then these institutions will start to change too.

Remember, too, that you are now keenly aware that the financial decision you make today, even though it is the best possible decision that could be made, will not necessarily be the best forevermore. Circumstances are constantly changing and, to create as much wealth as possible from your circumstances, all decisions need to be reviewed regularly. Tax rates and rules alter at least once a year; in Ireland, that happens on the first Wednesday of every December – we call it the Budget. Your circumstances will change too. At times, you will have more disposable income (and thus more money to invest), at other times, less. Hopefully, you now see that every single financial decision you make (whether to invest, save, borrow or spend money) has an impact on your entire financial world. Some financial decisions have the ability to draw you closer to your financial freedom (investments and savings) while others will push you in the opposite direction (borrowing for consumables: cars, holidays, shoes, etc – and spending in general).

You already know I do not contribute to the "self-denial-until-you-can-afford-to-live-like-a-king" school of thought, as I believe you need to enjoy the journey. However, I do believe that those decisions to spend frivolously need to be made in the context of your efforts to achieve financial freedom. For example, I met with a client recently who is well on the way to financial freedom, which is planned to be reached in five years' time when he is 54. He had fallen in love with an Aston Martin motor car and was seeking my input into the decision whether to buy. This was not a matter of whether he had the capacity to buy, he had, but what I told him was that the purchase would push financial freedom out a further four years. For this man, the cost was no longer the monthly outlay, it was a further four years of full-time work, a suspension of his and his wife's "retirement" plans and, in the end, he decided that was too high a price to pay.

Risk, and how to identify the true nature of it, has been discussed and, hopefully, you now understand investment risk that bit more than when you first picked up this book.

Investment risk is frightening, but the more you experience it, and the more you understand it, the less scary it will become. The ability to take investment risk is imperative, if you wish to create real financial freedom. Of course, there are always exceptions to every rule and I have no doubt that, if I looked hard enough, I could find someone who has become financially free without taking risk. However, such people are very much the exception and the truth is that the vast number of those who reach financial freedom do so by taking the necessary risks.

Knowing when you no longer need to take risk is just as important. When financial freedom is achieved, the need to take major risk (with the assets that can underwrite your financial security for the rest of your life) is no more. Investing to create income is a very different activity from investing to create wealth and, in my view, there is no potential reward that would make me risk my hard-won financial freedom.

Once financial freedom has been achieved, your financial focus should change to one of maintaining and, eventually, passing on your wealth. A properly constructed succession plan will protect your life's work from substantial erosion, when it is eventually inherited by the next generation. More importantly perhaps, it can protect your heirs from major legal battles and the emotional hurt and stress that such actions can cause. It can also serve to copper-fasten the value of those assets that depend upon you for that value, particularly relevant to those who own shares in private businesses.

Throughout this book, I have given examples of how certain planning interventions can improve the financial world of certain types of people. The manner in which you earn your income, the way you invest income that is surplus to lifestyle requirements, the methods you use to borrow and to repay those borrowings, all have been showcased here. But please do not confuse a demonstration with a recommendation. Even if your circumstances perfectly match the scenarios used in my examples, this does not automatically mean you should jump into action.

None of these actions will deliver the maximum benefit to you, unless and until they are taken as part of an overall, integrated plan. Another way of saying the same thing might be:

"Just because you can do something, does not necessarily mean you should."

Of course, the examples demonstrate that financial benefits come with a cost attaching and, in some cases (although not all, it has to be said), with an additional risk. In isolation, as long as the costs are justified by the benefits, then you might expect me to simply state that everyone should make the changes. However, such isolated thinking (and you are now all too aware of the problems that can be caused as isolated thinking allows inefficiencies to creep into your financial world) ignores the opportunity costs of taking the action. While you may receive a superior benefit, the fact remains that the same cost spent elsewhere may provide an even greater benefit and so all options available to you need to be considered.

Last, but by no means least, perhaps the greatest message of all to impart is that the alignment of goals is all-important. Ensuring that your financial adviser, your business partner(s) and even your romantic partner, have their goals aligned with your own will avoid conflicts in the future.

TRUST

One word that people often throw at me when I speak on this subject is "trust". Insisting that all financial advice you receive is in writing on the headed notepaper of the adviser (or the terms and conditions of a business partnership are contained in a legally-binding co-ownership agreement) can be interpreted by some as a demonstration of a lack of trust. However, it is not – in my view, it is simply a professional method of regulating the relationship and of protecting all parties as much as possible.

Indeed, in my own financial world, following an agreement to merge *Financial Engineering Network Ltd.* with another entity, we recently had to re-draft our co-ownership agreement. Despite the fact that our business employs many people with expertise in this specialist area, we chose to outsource the re-drafting to an independent legal firm and then all of the shareholders met to discuss the draft.

One clause in the first draft of that agreement was something I could not sign up to. In essence, it meant that my fellow shareholders could "manufacture" a situation where, if I quit the company without their blessing, I could lose up to 80% of my share value. Now, I could not envisage a scenario arising (and still cannot) where I would quit without agreement, nor could I imagine a situation where my fellow shareholders, whom I count amongst my closest friends, would deliberately work against me in this manner. However, just because I could not imagine such a scenario does not guarantee that it could never arise. My fellow shareholders are people in whom I place more trust than practically anyone else on the planet. I trust them on a daily basis with the money I have invested in my business. I have told my wife and family that they are the people to whom they should turn if I were to die suddenly. I have even asked a number of them to be godparents to my children and the executors of my will. This said, I have seen closer relationships than the one I share with my fellow shareholders destroyed over money and over considerably less money than the value of my stake-holding in our business. It is probably worth saying that I was pointing out this issue for the benefit of all the shareholders (the offending clause would have applied to us all) and, once I explained my objections. we all agreed that none of us would like to see that clause included.

There are very few people on this planet whom I trust so much as to be sure that, when presented with a particular financial decision to make, they would **always** make the decision that most benefited me, even to their own cost. Today, in fact, there are only four people in whom I would place that ultimate trust. The first three are my parents and my wife. Time and time again, they have proven to me that, even to their own detriment, they will make the decision that benefits me first. The fourth is my financial adviser, not because I hold him in the same esteem as my closest family, but because we have aligned our goals. What is good for me is good for him and *vice versa*. If he were to act in a manner that cost me money, it would cost him money too.

Of course, trusting one's advisers is very important. That is why I have recommended the in-depth analysis and investigations that should go into choosing (or re-choosing perhaps) your financial adviser. Just as important, in my view, is continuing to create (and continuing to insist upon) the environment that ensures the trust you do place in him/her is not taken for granted or, worst still, betrayed in some fashion. If this environment makes advisers uncomfortable in any way, my belief is that says much more about the advisers than it does about the person seeking the comfort that that environment provides.

I hope that you have enjoyed reading this book as much as I have enjoyed writing it and I wish you the very best of luck in any and all of your endeavours to create the exceptional financial future that true financial freedom can deliver.

Appendix I: The Cost of Annual Management Fees as a Percentage of the Amount Invested

Term	Annual Management Fee		
	0.5% pa	1% pa	1.5% pa
1	0.03%	0.56%	0.84%
5	1.54%	3.05%	4.54%
10	3.72%	7.31%	10.78%
15	6.81%	13.26%	19.39%
20	11.14%	21.50%	31.15%
25	17.16%	32.82%	47.13%
30	25.48%	48.28%	68.70%

Note: All figures rounded to two decimal points. All other management fees will be proportionate.

This table illustrates (based on the maximum gross growth rate used for illustration purposes by Irish fund management businesses, currently 6% *p.a.*) the cost of the annual management fee as a percentage of the money you invest. For example, investing €100,000 over 15 years in a fund with a 1% *p.a.* management fee and producing a gross growth rate of 6% *p.a.* costs you €13,260. Investing the same €100,000 over 20 years in a fund producing a gross growth of 6% *p.a.* and with a management fee of 1.5% *p.a.* costs you €31,150.

While some may argue that quoting a fee levied on the investment fund as a percentage of the investment amount is unfair (unfair to the fund management/insurance/banking industry that is), I do not contribute to that argument. The only way, in my view, to judge value for money for the investor is this way. Your only benchmark is the amount of money you part with and, thus, judging charges as a percentage of that amount perfectly illustrates the value for money being provided.

It is important that, as you view this table, you recognise that different funds will have higher (some even higher than those illustrated) or lower annual management fees and that this fee directly influences the wealth you create. For example, a fund that charges 1.5% *p.a.* will have to outperform the fund charging 0.5% *p.a.* by more than 1% *p.a.* before paying the extra fee would be worth your while.

Now that you have read the book, why not enter a draw to win a FREE day of Financial Coaching with Paul Overy?

Paul Overy left the employment of Financial Engineering Ltd in March 2008 to concentrate exclusively on Financial Coaching, which he is delivering either on a one-to-one basis or to groups as part of their employer's efforts to provide a superior compensation package.

To celebrate the launch of this, his second, financial book, Paul is offering all readers the opportunity to win a *FREE* day of Financial Coaching, on a one-to-one basis, with himself. Each month, up to 31 December 2008, everyone who completes and returns the form overleaf to Oak Tree Press at 19 Rutland Street, Cork will be included in a draw.

This opportunity is only available to entrants who live and work in the Republic of Ireland.

I wish to be entered into a draw to win a **FREE** day of Financial Coaching with Paul Overy.

Name	
Home address	
Business address	
Email	
Preferred contact phone number(s)	
Occupation	

Feedback on *The Tactics of the Rich* is most welcome. Please make any comments here:

I understand that, once this application is received by Oak Tree Press, I will be entered into the draw that takes place that month. I also understand that, if I win the monthly prize of a free day's Financial Coaching with Paul Overy, the free day consists of 8 hours at a venue of my choosing and that the 8 hours includes Paul's travel time to and from the venue I choose.

Signature: _____

Paul Overy would like to add your name to his mailing list, so that you will receive communications about the services of his new business. If you do wish to receive marketing material, please tick this box ☐

If you commented on *The Tactics of the Rich* in the feedback box above, Paul Overy would like permission to use those comments in future marketing initiatives. If you are willing to grant him permission to use your comments (which would not name you personally, but would appear in the format of "*Mr/Ms A, Anytown*"), then please tick this box ☐

OAK TREE PRESS

is Ireland's leading business book publisher.

It develops and delivers
information, advice and resources
to entrepreneurs and managers –
and those who educate and support them.

Its print, software and web materials
are in use in Ireland, the UK, Finland,
Greece, Norway and Slovenia.

❖

OAK TREE PRESS
19 Rutland Street
Cork, Ireland
T: + 353 21 4313855
F: + 353 21 4313496
E: info@oaktreepress.com
W: www.oaktreepress.com